Instructor's Manual and Audioscript

to accompany

LE FRANÇAIS Départ-Arrivée

FOURTH EDITION

John A. Rassias
Dartmouth College

Jacqueline de La Chapelle Skubly
Housatonic Community College

Joel D. Goldfield
Fairfield University

with Kathleen Kinnaman

Dartmouth College Press
Published by University Press of New England,
One Court Street, Lebanon, NH 03766
www.upne.com

Originally published in 1992 by Heinle & Heinle Publishers
Printed in the United States of America
5 4 3 2 1

TABLE DES MATIERES

Instructor's Manual

The main purposes of *LE FRANÇAIS: Départ-Arrivée,* Fourth Edition, are to lead students to communicate in French and to appreciate the francophone world. Each feature of the text is designed to prepare students to attain these goals. This *Instructor's Manual* is intended to explain procedures we follow in class, to give you hints on how to handle specific items, and to supplement the many communicative exercises (such as the **Travaux pratiques**) in the text and in the *Student Workbook/Laboratory Manual.*

The structure of each chapter—with the exception of the **Chapitre préliminaire, Chapitre 1,** and the **Chapitre facultatif**—is the same. Each contains

1. An illustration that captures the essence of the **Scénario**
2. An **Itinéraire** that maps out the ground to be covered
3. A **Scénario** in three **étapes**
4. **Questions sur le scénario**
5. **Coin culturel** (cultural information, gestures, and proverbs)
6. **Vocabulaire illustré**
7. **Allons plus loin** (extension of chapter themes and vocabulary)
8. Five **Notes de grammaire**
9. A variety of controlled exercises
10. **Travaux pratiques** (activities that encourage students' creativity)
11. **Micrologues** (short cultural and informative passages)
12. **Lectures** (from **Chapitre 5** on)
13. **Création et récréation** (chapter-ending synthesizing activities)
14. **Coup d'œil** (systematic chapter review)
15. **Vocabulaire**

This *Instructor's Manual* attempts to channel your energy and your activities so that they will be productive. Through the proper use of this manual it will be possible to create an air of spontaneity for each class you teach. The most effective kind of spontaneity is the rehearsed kind that, as the actor and playwright William Gillette put it, allows us "to create the illusion of the first time."

Language learning should not be tedious; it should be fun. Instructor and students should cooperate in the learning process. The more we offer our students by way of material and approaches, the more eagerly they will pick up the challenge.

A final word about using the text and the *Instructor's Manual:* We do not presume to tell you how to teach. Essentially, we have mapped an approach in this manual to bring the best out of the text. The teaching aids are merely suggestions you may want to use.

Typical Lesson Plan

A typical lesson requires approximately four and a half hours to complete, including time for testing.

Day One

1. Presentation of the **Scénario (Première** and **Deuxième étapes)**
2. Reading of the **Troisième étape** (optional)
3. **Questions sur le scénario**
4. **Coin culturel**
5. **Vocabulaire illustré**

Day Two

1. **Allons plus loin**
2. **Note de grammaire 1**
3. Exercises
4. **Note de grammaire 2**
5. Exercises

Day Three

1. **Note de grammaire 3**
2. Exercises
3. **Note de grammaire 4**
4. Exercises
5. **Note de grammaire 5**

Day Four

1. Review of **Note de grammaire 5**
2. Exercises
3. **Micrologue** and questions
4. **Lecture**
5. **Création et récréation**
6. **Coup d'œil**

Day Five

1. Test
2. Review of previous lesson
3. Presentation of the new chapter's **Scénario (Première** and **Deuxième étapes)**
4. Etc.

The amount and variety of material in the text allow maximum flexibility. Certain sections of each chapter may readily be assigned as homework and treated as recognition exercises, such as the **Coin culturel** text (but not the **Gestes** and **Proverbes**, which must be acted out) and the **Allons plus loin.** In addition, some of the features listed in the typical lesson plan as in-class activities may be assigned as homework.

Approach to Each Lesson

Students are in your class for various reasons, such as to fulfill a requirement, to see what language study is all about, to learn a language because of ethnic background, or to prepare for a vocation or travel. Whatever reasons draw students to language classes, only good instruction will keep them there. Appropriate materials help keep their interest alive, but ultimately it is effective teaching that keeps them enthusiastic about learning.

I should like to share some hints on approaching each lesson.

Chapitre préliminaire

1. After a general introduction to the course, present yourself to the class: **Bonjour. Je m'appelle M./Mme/Mlle** ________. Introduce yourself to each student, giving each one a quick handshake. From the very beginning, incorporate culturally based gestures into your presentation. The French handshake is a brisk, single pump of the hand. Students will immediately notice the difference from the American manner of making introductions.

Establish that you will speak French as much as possible in class and that English will be reserved for those instances in which it is absolutely necessary to avoid confusion or to save time.

Repeat: **Je m'appelle ________**. Then ask the question: **Comment vous appelez-vous?** The student should answer appropriately. Be patient if the response is not immediate and use gestures to get the point across. Once the student responds correctly, express your pleasure enthusiastically. Ask each student what his/her name is.

Once this exercise has been mastered, point to a student and say: **Il/Elle s'appelle ________**. Then ask the question: **Comment s'appelle-t-il/elle?** Have the neighbor of each student respond to the question.

2. As an introduction to language, we offer simple hints to ease the transition from English to French. The French alphabet is introduced and accents are presented. Suggestions for determining gender are also provided, as are practical expressions that should be acted out by every student in the class. Finally, pairs of students should work on the **Travaux pratiques** that accompany the classroom vocabulary in the **Allons plus loin.**

It would be well to spend as much time as possible on the **Chapitre préliminaire,** perhaps two days, to ensure that students feel completely at ease with the material, understand simple commands, can identify classroom objects, and recognize simple French.

One way of putting students at ease is to show them that every sound we utter conveys a meaning, as does every movement of our bodies. For instance, select two students and tell them to convey their feelings and emotions using only the alphabet they have just learned plus gestures and intonations. One condition: they must use the alphabet in sequence, proceeding from a to z. Or they may act out a situation, such as one student who wants a favor from another student, who is reluctant to cooperate. Again, the only means of communication is through the alphabet. Student A tries to be pleasant: **a, b, c;** Student B responds, reluctantly: **d, e, f.** Student A tries again: **g, h?;** Student B answers nervously: **i, j, k, l.** Student A tries again: **m, n, o, p;** Student B now says angrily: **q, r, s!** Student A realizes that nothing is to be gained: **t, u, v;** Student B, pleased that Student A has understood, says agreeably: **x, y, z!**

Also, each student should spell his or her name in French, while another writes the letters on the board. As they do so, make sure that they give double letters as **deux s, deux f,** etc.

3. Expressions utiles. Read and perform each command for the class. Then have students take turns giving commands to other students, who must perform appropriately. Make sure that the entire class participates, and volunteer to receive commands yourself.

4. Before I dismiss the class, I present a monologue in French, taken from any author (for example, La Fontaine or Diderot). Initially, I mime the passage. Then I present it verbally along with the mime. The purpose is to show students what they themselves will be able to do and that language is an art form that involves a person's entire being. It is crucial that students see for themselves that verb conjugations and memorization ultimately lead somewhere.

Chapitre 1: Le départ

The organization of this chapter varies from the standard organization of succeeding chapters.

1. Pre-cognition text. The first five chapters are introduced by pre-cognition texts that appear only in this manual. These texts situate and introduce the **Scénarios** and should be read to the students while their books are open to the illustration that begins each chapter. Before you begin to work with the text itself, tell students to open their books: **Ouvrez vos livres!** Say the page number of the chapter-opening illustration in French and write the number on the chalkboard. Read the following pre-cognition text to the students as they look at the illustration. The pre-cognition text is intended to show that French uses many English cognates.

> Deux Américains désirent continuer leurs études de français en France. Ils voyagent ensemble. Ils sont contents d'aller en France pour étudier et, bien sûr, pour s'amuser.

Try to dramatize the sense of the pre-cognition reading. If students do not understand the general sense of the text *after* one or two readings, explain it in English.

2. Première étape. Have students look at the illustration while you read them the **Première étape.** Because the goal of the **Première étape** is comprehension, read it aloud several times, but do not ask the students to repeat. This section isolates some of the basic elements of the **Scénario.**

3. Deuxième étape. Books are now closed. Read the entire **Deuxième étape** aloud, being as dramatic as possible. Dramatization is an effective way of presenting this material because it provides an opportunity to demonstrate cultural nuances. And in all cases, your students will appreciate the effort. After the pantomime, present the text line by line using backward build-up—that is, presenting each sentence in breath groups, beginning with the last breath group in the sentence and building toward the first. (For further instruction on backward build-up, please turn to page IM-30.)

4. Troisième étape. This **étape,** which brings the **Première** and **Deuxième étapes** into focus and adds some new lexical items, is an optional feature designed for reading only. If you decide to use this **étape,** explain new vocabulary to students and have them practice substituting **Synonymes et expressions approximatives** from the *Student Workbook/Laboratory Manual.*

5. Vocabulaire illustré. Have students keep their books open as you read the words and point to the pictures. The illustrations prevent the student from first associating the words with their English equivalents.

6. Faisons connaissance. Pointing to the chapter-opening illustration, identify the characters. Then state: **Je m'appelle** ________. Identify other students in the class and ask others to name them. Then, still working with the introductory illustrations, ask how Henry and Robert are. State how you feel: **Je vais bien.** Then ask each student: **Comment allez-vous?**

7. Note de grammaire 1: Les pronoms personnels sujets. Note that all grammar notes are presented in the simplest manner possible. It may be helpful to have students consult the **Glossary of Grammatical Terms** in the appendices to familiarize themselves with basic terminology.

To teach the personal pronouns, point to yourself and say **je.** Point to a student and say **tu** in a way that shows close acquaintanceship, such as by giving him or her a "high-five" sign. (This may be a good time to show the relative nature and applicability of gestures in at least one francophone country. For instance, in Senegal the handshake is a prolonged pumping that continues while participants ask after members of each other's families.) Then point to appropriate individuals and indicate **il, elle. Nous** may be illustrated by including yourself in a group of students. The formal **vous** may be shown by shaking a student's hand formally. The plural **vous** is shown by addressing a group of people. **Ils** is demonstrated by pointing to a group of males, **elles** is shown by pointing to a group of females, and the combined sexes are indicated by addressing them as **ils. On** could be introduced separately by pointing in a vague manner to a student (indicating "one") and to the whole group in the same general way.

8. Substitution and transformation drills. The need constantly arises to check whether individuals or the class as a whole has grasped the sense of what we are doing. Verification techniques vary according to the situation. We use substitution and transformation drills to put students at ease with the language and check basic control. Such drills play a well-defined and restricted role in the total presentation. However, we do not view these as routine, mindless repetition exercises, but rather as minidramas that provide a script for instructor and students to perform. Drills help students acquire the tools of language more rapidly than any other technique. The amount of drilling in a regular class hour need average no more than ten minutes. Bear in mind, however, that the energy that goes into such practice sparks full-class participation and establishes a rhythm that enhances language learning and the immediate grasp of cultural peculiarities. We believe that it is after students have acquired the rudiments of language and cultural patterns that communication takes place. A special section on presentation techniques for substitution and transformation drills appears on pages 31 and 32 of this manual.

9. Note de grammaire 2: Le verbe irrégulier *être*. It's fun to present the verb **être** by citing Hamlet's **Etre ou ne pas être.** The verb is presented with the subject pronoun, following the same steps as in Step 7 above. Simple substitutions reinforce the manipulation of the pronoun and the verb.

10. Note de grammaire 3: Le verbe irrégulier *aller*. The verb **aller** is introduced in the context of the **Scénario.** It may be explained by saying **Je vais à la porte/à la chaise/au**

tableau/à la fenêtre, etc., while performing each action. I recommend that all verbs be introduced by acting them out.

11. Note de grammaire 4: Les articles définis et indéfinis. The use of the definite and indefinite articles may be illustrated by saying **L'avion de New York arrive à 10 heures,** stressing the specificity of the airplane from New York. The indefinite article may be presented by saying **Un avion arrive ici toutes les heures.**

Point out that the **h** in French is never pronounced and that the mute **h** is considered a vowel, while the aspirate **h** is a consonant.

12. Note de grammaire 5: Interrogations. All the basic ways of asking questions are presented here. We take this approach for two reasons: (1) the procedures are not difficult, and (2) they illustrate that French grammar rules are controllable and do not have many exceptions. Such knowledge should build students' confidence.

A series of transformation drills reinforce this material. Note that the drills in this book are often accompanied by structural cues that emphasize their focus and thus help students concentrate their energies.

13. Arbre généalogique de Christophe. To help students speak more about themselves and acquire essential vocabulary, we present the genealogical tree of a French family. Students' books should be open for this exercise. Point to the relationships and emphasize the new words. The exercises help students transfer the vocabulary from the textbook to their personal situations.

14. Questions sur le scénario. In this first chapter the questions on the **Scénario** appear at the end of the exercises. This postponement gives students a chance to acquire as many structures as possible to incorporate into their responses. Encourage students to answer fully. Most questions are in the **vous** form.

15. Création et récréation. This section is intended to motivate students to use French creatively and have fun in the process. Students should be encouraged to bring in photos of their own families to discuss. It is also advisable to have a variety of photos available for students who do not have any of their own.

Throughout the book we follow Monique Golaud and Pierre Dubout, two French students who spend a term studying in the United States. This device allows students to look at life in the United States as it may be seen through French eyes. The sections dealing with Monique and Pierre may be done orally in class or as homework.

16. Coup d'œil. This section provides a complete review of the main grammatical elements presented in the chapter. Students may indicate whether they have grasped a grammatical element by placing a check mark in either the **OUI** or the **NON** column. A check in the **NON** column means that the student should reread the appropriate section and ask questions until he/she has gained mastery.

In addition to serving as a review tool, the **Coup d'œil** may be used to introduce a chapter's grammar. In some classes I have used an elongated thermometer—the kind often seen in United Way fund raising—to indicate day-by-day progress in gaining control of target structures. Psychologically, this demonstrates that it is possible to learn French both thoroughly and quickly. To construct such a "thermometer of learning," list the various points in the **Coup d'œil,** starting with **Chapitre 1** at the bottom and continuing upward.

17. Vocabulaire. Wherever possible, words are grouped by themes to facilitate learning.

18. Supplementary vocabulary. Useful terms to teach at this time are **point** (period), **virgule** (comma), **point-virgule** (semicolon), **deux-points** (colon), **point d'interrogation** (question mark), **point d'exclamation** (exclamation point).

Chapitre 2: L'arrivée

1. Review. Before proceeding with **Chapitre 2,** check students' mastery of **Chapitre 1** by asking them to present the **Deuxième étape** of **Chapitre 1** as a dramatic skit. Encourage them to be imaginative. Assume the responsibility of "staging" the productions or appoint a **metteur en scène** who will be in charge of the **mise en scène.** The **metteur en scène** will choose the actors and actresses, designate others to make sound effects, and appoint yet someone else to serve as the **souffleur.** After one version, appoint another **metteur en scène**

to mount a second presentation, following the same procedures. Gender need have no bearing on the assignment of roles.

A second way to measure mastery is to ask students to recite the **Scénario,** providing them with occasional cues. Accept any appropriate responses, even if they are not exactly as shown in the text.

Still another way to encourage the class to capture the spirit of the **Scénario** is to have a group of students create a parallel version of the story line or to interpret the dialogue in a different setting. As the term progresses, encourage students to incorporate past **Scénarios** into the new material.

2. Make sure that everyone has filled out the checklist accompanying the preceding **Coup d'œil.** If there are any points that students still do not understand, clear them up before beginning **Chapitre 2.**

3. Pre-cognition text. To begin the new lesson, read the pre-cognition text for this chapter while students look at the chapter-opening illustration:

> Le jet arrive à Paris et les trois Américains cherchent leurs bagages. Ils désirent un taxi pour aller à la gare où il y a les trains. Le chauffeur de taxi n'est pas patient.

Read this passage twice, trying to dramatize its sense as much as possible. Then proceed along the lines discussed in **Chapitre 1** for the presentation of the three **étapes.**

4. Vocabulaire pour les questions. Read these terms aloud to the class, emphasizing their formulaic nature.

5. Questions sur le scénario. These questions incorporate the new question vocabulary. Encourage students to answer fully.

6. Coin culturel. These sections expand on cultural themes presented in the chapter. Students should act out the gestures and demonstrate their American equivalents, if they exist. The proverbs should be memorized.

7. Note de grammaire 6: Le verbe *avoir*. The present tense of **avoir** is presented in full. Make sure that students distinguish between the third person plural forms of **être** and **avoir: ils sont** and **ils ont.**

8. Note de grammaire 7: Les verbes réguliers en *-er*. It would be well to allocate as much time as possible to the study of verbs. In presenting regular **-er** verbs, point out that the box around the first, second, and third persons singular and the third person plural indicates that these forms are all pronounced alike. The boxing of identically pronounced verb forms is a regular feature of this text which also appears—whenever appropriate—with irregular verbs.

Emphasize the three ways the present tense may be translated into English. For example, **je parle** = *I speak, I do speak, I am speaking.*

Students should be able to handle the present tense of all verbs ending in **-er** without difficulty. Point out that the vast majority of French verbs end in **-er** and that one need only know the meaning of an infinitive to put it to full use. Point out that verbs like **amuser, continuer, décider, désirer, dîner, intimider, irriter,** and **voyager** are cognates. Also warn against **faux amis.**

9. Note de grammaire 8: Les nombres cardinaux. The numbers from 0 to 20 are presented with a variety of exercises. One way to provide further practice is to use dice. To begin, roll the dice and ask students to call out the totals. For simple addition you may roll one, two, or three dice. After the addition exercises, have students multiply the dots on two dice. You may also want students to continue the activity in small groups, correcting each other as necessary. Emphasize that speed counts in this drill.

Another game, ("Connect the Dots"), may be done on the chalkboard. Arrange numbered dots to spell out a word that is particularly meaningful to the group, such as the name of your school or city. This will require some preclass preparation. The numbers should be randomized and linked in pairs. Read off pairs of numbers in French and have students connect the two points. Do not follow a strict order, but go from letter to letter, joining two dots each time. This activity should last five to ten minutes. These drills are done so fast that the students respond without thinking of quantities in English and then translating them into French.

10. Note de grammaire 9: L'heure. Drill telling time by asking as many questions as possible about everyday events—for instance, **A quelle heure déjeunez-vous?** or **A quelle heure la classe se termine-t-elle?**

Bring a clock with a large dial to class. Identify it as **la pendule.** Indicate the hours and minutes you want the students to say. I often have a student serve as a human clock, placing his/her hands to indicate the times called out by students.

11. Note de grammaire 10: Ne... pas. Some students become confused because they consider **ne... pas** a double negative. One way to dispell such a notion is to point out that this expression in fact contains one negative element (**ne**) and one affirmative element (**pas**), and that the second element was once a noun. I tell my students that the first person in French who made a negative statement using **ne... pas** intended to say that he/she would not yield by a step (**un pas**).

Negative questions are constructed similarly to regular questions, with the negating particles surrounding the verb and the pronoun subject. To reinforce this point beyond the material presented in the text, you may ask the students to negate all the possible verbs in the first dialogue. Some of the results may be interesting.

Emphasize that the only time that **si** means "yes" is when it is used as an affirmative answer to a negative question.

12. Arbre généalogique. The genealogical tree is expanded to show additional family relationships and the ages of the children. A good exercise would be to have the students sketch and discuss their own genealogical trees, as suggested in the **Création et récréation.**

13. Micrologue. A **Micrologue** is essentially a one-minute passage about a subject of cultural interest that may be used in various ways. It makes an ideal brief reading selection or discussion generator. Another approach is to use the **Micrologue** as a speed-writing drill. Begin by selecting three students. Student A's task is to listen carefully each time the **Micrologue** is read and to answer questions later. Student B will write the **Micrologue** on the chalkboard, preferably out of sight of the rest of the class. And Student C will act as timekeeper. Select a time limit for the reading of the **Micrologue** (say, 90 seconds) and insist that the timekeeper stop you each time that limit is reached.

The **Micrologue** will be read three times. The first time, all students will listen carefully. The second time, all students except Students A and C will write what they hear. Emphasize that students should try to write as many words as they can grasp and should not worry if they catch only a few here and there. (Note that this procedure is much more relaxed than a traditional **dictée** in that students are not expected to catch every word.) On the third reading, all students but A and C should correct what they have written.

Be sure to respect the timekeeper's orders each time the **Micrologue** is read. If he/she says "Stop!" you should do so immediately, even if you are in the middle of a word or sentence. Once the **Micrologue** has been read three times, Student C's responsibilities are fulfilled and attention turns to Student A.

Begin by clarifying the vocabulary of the **Micrologue,** using visual aids if necessary and appropriate. Then ask Student A to repeat the **Micrologue,** quoting verbatim when possible and paraphrasing the rest of the time. Coach Student A through words and phrases he or she can't recall and end the exercise with enthusiastic congratulations.

You may ask Student A to repeat the **Micrologue** a day or two (or even a week or more) later. Due to the cumulative effect of language learning, he or she will invariably modify and expand the original text.

This entire activity should take about ten minutes, with an additional two minutes to correct the text (or notes) Student B has written on the chalkboard. You may also make up your own **Micrologues,** which will expose students to cultural information not available in other texts.

14. Création et récréation. These activities may be done orally in class or prepared as homework and then read to the class.

15. Coup d'œil. Go over the **Coup d'œil** for review or assign it for homework.

16. The Wave. Isolate the verbs presented in this chapter through a technique I call a "Wave." Select certain new verbs, such as **voler, arriver, chercher, verifier,** and **trouver,** and designate students to incorporate these verbs into a short skit. To illustrate, you may create the following scenario, assigning one sentence to each student:

1. Je **voyage** dans un avion.
2. J'**arrive** en France.

3. Je **cherche** mes bagages.
4. Un agent de police **vérifie** mon passeport.
5. Je **trouve** un taxi.

Student 1 says sentence 1 and acts out flying in an airplane. Student 2 repeats sentence 1, along with his or her version of flying and adds sentence 2, acting out arriving on French soil. Student 3 acts out and repeats the sentences of the first two students and then looks for his/her baggage. Student 4 acts out and repeats all preceding sentences and then, with bags in hand, states that a customs officer checks his/her passport. Finally, Student 5 acts out and repeats all preceding verbs and hails a taxi.

Later in the term you may choose to assign this as homework. Students will write out sentences using the verbs you assign and then present the scenario to the class the following day.

Chapitre 3: A la gare

1. Pre-cognition text. Review the preceding chapter using the procedures in Steps 1–2 of **Chapitre 2.** Then proceed to the **Scénario.** The precognition text for this chapter is:

> Après la première mésaventure, les trois amis arrivent à la gare à neuf heures moins le quart. Ils achètent trois billets, mais l'employé est aussi impatient que le chauffeur de taxi.

2. Coin culturel. Students should act out the gestures in each chapter and then demonstrate the equivalent American sign, if it exists. The proverbs should be memorized.

3. Vocabulaire illustré. To practice the new vocabulary, have teams of students identify and incorporate the appropriate emotions in their renditions of the **Scénario.**

4. Note de grammaire 11: Les prépositions *à* et *de* et les articles définis. Students often have difficulty in grasping the contractions of the masculine singular forms and the plural forms. Insist on this point.

5. Note de grammaire 12: Les nombres cardinaux à partir de 20. The numbers may be reinforced using the dice and dots techniques described in **Chapitre 2,** Step 11. Intensify the game by speeding up each roll of the dice and by asking for rapid additions, multiplications, or subtractions. This is also a good time to play bingo in French.

6. Le calendrier. You may prefer to postpone work with the calendar until after **Note de grammaire 13** has been completed. Have the students study the calendar. Point out the typical French traits of this calendar: the days named after saints and Monday as the first day of the week. Assign the cultural notes that accompany the calendar as homework.

Every student should be able to give the day of his/her birth, name day, year of birth, etc, and the birth dates of the people in his/her family tree.

As a study in comparative culture, assign two students to discuss the differences between an American calendar and a French calendar and to compare and contrast the most important holidays in the United States and France.

7. Note de grammaire 13: Les jours, les mois, les saisons et les dates. Practice the new concepts in this section using a rotation drill. Name a day of the week, a month, a season, or an hour and have a student supply the next three items in the sequence:

INSTRUCTOR: vendredi
STUDENT: samedi, dimanche, lundi
INSTRUCTOR: février
STUDENT: mars, avril, mai
INSTRUCTOR: le printemps
STUDENT: l'été, l'automne, l'hiver
INSTRUCTOR: une heure cinq
STUDENT: deux heures cinq, trois heures cinq, quatre heures cinq

Ask students: **En quel mois êtes-vous né(e)? C'est en quelle saison? Et tes parents? Tes grands-parents?** etc.

8. Note de grammaire 14: L'heure officielle. Much like the drill on regular time, bring in a clock with a large dial and have students identify the hour shown, this time stating both regular and official times. Have students study the official railroad timetable and interpret hours in both regular and official times. Have them estimate how long the trip lasts.

9. Exercice de compréhension. This cartoon from *Tintin* centers on the Dupondt brothers' confusion of the hour. It brings lively action and fresh language into the course.

10. Note de grammaire 15: Le futur immédiat. Reinforce both the immediate future and the present by starting a story and asking students to continue it as logically as possible. Begin in the present tense and designate the student who is to continue it by tossing a soft handball to him/her. That student adds a sentence, then determines the next speaker by tossing the ball to him/her. If someone makes a mistake, the person to whom he/she tosses the ball should signal the error by tossing the ball back. After thorough review of the present, switch to the immediate future.

11. Travaux pratiques. Activities like this serve as important verification drills. It is obvious that if the students can ask and answer these questions, they know the target material. Encourage students to respond quickly and fully.

12. Micrologue. Follow instructions for **Chapitre 2,** Step 13. This one, which is devoted to cities, demonstrates how students may adapt such texts directly to their own needs.

13. Création et récréation. If time permits, do a Wave as a supplemental exercise. Assign one of the following adjectives to each of five students: **bouleversé(e), déconcerté(e), désorienté(e), impatient(e), occupé(e).** Student 1 mimes **bouleversé(e),** Student 2 repeats the mime and then adds his/her own adjective, and so on, until the last student in the group, who must act out all five adjectives as a dramatic presentation.

Remind students that the story of Monique and Pierre continues from chapter to chapter.

14. Coup d'œil. Verify whether the **Coup d'œil** has been done.

Chapitre 4: Dans le train

1. Pre-cognition text. Follow the review procedures in Steps 1–2 of **Chapitre 2.** Then proceed to the **Scénario.** The pre-cognition text for this chapter is:

> Les trois amis se demandent si tous les Français sont brusques et impatients. Un vieux monsieur entre dans le même compartiment et il répond à leurs questions. Il est gentil.

2. By now students should be curious to know other ways of saying some of the terms they have been learning. The **Synonymes et expressions approximatives** sections in the *Student Workbook/Laboratory Manual* provide alternative expressions they can incorporate in their personalized versions of the **Scénarios.**

3. Coin culturel. Assign the **Coin culturel** as homework. Ask one student to prepare a short presentation comparing trains in the United States with those in France.

4. Vocabulaire illustré. When teaching the names of animals, you may want to add others, such as **le lion, le tigre, l'éléphant, la girafe, le crocodile.**

5. Note de grammaire 16: Les adjectifs démonstratifs. These do not pose great problems for students, so relatively little time need be spent on them.

6. Note de grammaire 17: L'impératif. As a review and lead-in, have one student repeat all the commands presented in **Chapitre préliminaire, Expressions utiles,** while other students act them out.

7. Note de grammaire 18: Le verbe *faire*. As you discuss the verb **faire,** emphasize its wide use in French.

8. Note de grammaire 19: Le temps et la météo. Once the class has learned weather expressions, a different student should be assigned to give a brief weather report for your region each day. This should be done immediately after review of the previous day's lesson. Students should be encouraged to bring in cut-outs representing the sun, rain, an umbrella, snow, etc. If a felt board is available, it would enhance the visuals accompanying the weather report. Obviously, the chalkboard will also do. Eventually, you may begin each class by having a rotation of students give brief updates of the news of the day, weather, and sports—the entire enterprise not to exceed five minutes.

To reinforce the infinitives of the three verbs used with weather, present them in the immediate future: **Il va pleuvoir/Il va neiger/Il va geler.**

9. Note de grammaire 20: Les verbes réguliers en *-ir*. We introduce **-ir** verbs relatively early in order to give the student more choices for self-expression. Once students have grasped how to conjugate **-er** verbs, they should have no problem in handling **-ir** verbs. This approach brings students closer to speaking real language, which enhances self-image and motivates learning.

10. Travaux pratiques. As a supplement to Exercise B, do a Wave using the terms **avoir peur, choisir, chuchoter, grandir,** and **grossir.** Following the format described in **Chapitre 2,** Step 16, Student 1 mimes and uses **avoir peur** in the sentence. Student 2 repeats the sentence and the mime and then adds his/her own sentence, and so on, until the last student in the group, who must do all five sentences as a dramatic presentation. This could also be done as a homework assignment, with each student preparing a scenario that contains all five expressions.

11. Micrologue. Follow instructions for the use of the **Micrologue** in **Chapitre 2,** Step 13.

12. Coup d'œil. The **Coups d'œil** become more and more valuable as we progress through the text. Students may refer to them at any point, check their knowledge, and adapt them to their own needs whenever appropriate.

Chapitre 5: Rencontre à la gare

1. Pre-cognition text. Follow the review procedures described in Steps 1–2 of **Chapitre 2.** Then proceed to the **Scénario.** The pre-cognition text for this chapter is:

> Quand les trois amis arrivent à la gare, ils font la connaissance de leurs familles françaises. Il y a beaucoup de monde à la gare. Tout le monde parle en même temps. Il y a un grand brouhaha et beaucoup de confusion.

2. Deuxième étape. During work on the **Deuxième étape,** ask students to incorporate elements from previous dialogues to create a more realistic situation. For instance, Robert could confide to Henry that he is **intimidé** by the scene at the station, or Henry could say that the families are **gentilles.**

3. Troisième étape. Have students read the **Troisième étape,** replacing the words in the text with the appropriate **Synonymes et expressions approximatives** in the *Student Workbook/Laboratory Manual.* This may become a regular activity as you concentrate more and more on reading as a regular exercise.

4. Vocabulaire illustré. To reinforce spatial relationships and directions, blindfold a student (or yourself) and have another student guide him/her (or you) to a specific place through a maze created by the class.

5. Note de grammaire 21: Le pluriel des noms et des adjectifs. Focus only on the rules presented. Do not burden students with the many exceptions to these rules.

6. Note de grammaire 22: Les adjectifs possessifs. Students may confuse agreement with the subject and the gender of the possessive adjective. Insist that agreement occurs *only* with the noun being modified.

7. Note de grammaire 23: Expressions avec *avoir*. The verb **avoir** has occurred in every chapter, along with some of its idiomatic uses. Students may now combine some weather expressions with the **avoir** expressions here. For instance, the following rotation drill is possible:

> Quand il fait froid, j'ai froid et j'aime le thé chaud.
> Quand il fait chaud, j'ai chaud et j'aime l'eau fraîche.
> Quand il neige,...; Quand il pleut,...; Quand il fait du soleil,...; Quand il gèle,...

Accept any response which makes sense.

8. Note de grammaire 24: Les verbes *voir* et *croire*. Voir, along with **prévoir,** are not difficult. Teach the saying « **Voir c'est croire!** » *"Seeing is believing!"*

9. Note de grammaire 25: *Venir* et *venir de* + infinitif. Venir is another high-frequency verb that should be mastered early in French language instruction. To establish the difference in meaning between **venir** and **venir de** + *infinitive,* line up three students. Class members give each student an infinitive and a tense which he/she must use in a sentence. When the student uses the immediate past tense, he/she takes a step back; when the present tense is used, the student maintains his/her place on the line; and when the future tense is used, the student takes one step forward. For instance, if a classmate suggests the verb **voir,** Student 1 may offer one of three responses, depending on the tense required:

Je viens voir mon ami(e). (*stays on the line*)
Je viens de voir mon ami(e). (*takes one step backward*)
Je vais voir mon ami(e). (*takes one step forward*)

Play continues with different verbs and tenses being offered to each student.

10. Micrologue. After students read the **Micrologue** about the subway system in France, have them compare that system with the subway systems in some large American cities.

11. Lecture. This is the first formal reading in the book. Students enjoy Prévert and appreciate how he manipulates language. This poem may be acted out by students, who read it with proper intonations.

12. Création et récréation. The Monique and Pierre episode must be done thoroughly.

13. Coup d'œil. Like all others, this **Coup d'œil** should be carefully completed. By now, students should be able to assess their own strengths and weaknesses.

14. Vocabulaire. To review vocabulary, ask a student to create a **Vocabulaire illustré** on the chalkboard by first drawing a huge circle. As students in class call out facial features, the first student draws them on the circle until the face of a person is obtained. Target vocabulary would include **la barbe, la bouche, la chevelure, les cheveux, le front, le menton, la moustache, le nez, les yeux, les oreilles.**

Then have other students direct the student to erase those features which a female student does not have, such as **la barbe** and **la moustache.**

15. Another way to review vocabulary is to write the following table of words on the board and ask students to identify the item that does not belong to each numbered group:

	A	B	C	D	E
1.	bouche	yeux	menton	nez	moustache
2.	garage	pharmacie	escalier	épicerie	gymnase
3.	venir	finir	tenir	maintenir	obtenir
4.	à l'heure	à temps	l'heure pile	anniversaire	l'heure tapante

Students should have eliminated 1 E, 2 C, 3 B, 4 D.

This exercise format may be used throughout the text. Later, students may be asked to define each item in simple terms.

16. One by one, ask students their names: **Comment vous appelez-vous?** Then ask if the student has a nickname **(un sobriquet)** and what its source is. Ask what name each student would prefer, if he/she had to choose a different name. Why?

Chapitre 6: Chez les Fourchet

1. Scénario. Students should no longer need pre-cognition texts. From this chapter on, procedures for beginning a new chapter and presenting the **Scénarios** are essentially the same as those suggested in **Chapitre 1,** Steps 2–4, and **Chapitre 2,** Steps 1–2. Any special variations will be presented in the appropriate chapter.

2. Vocabulaire illustré. Test students' mastery of these terms by asking them to draw a room on the chalkboard and fill it with appropriately labeled furnishings. The exercise may be varied by having a student direct the placement of the furniture—for instance: **Placez l'armoire derrière le lit, la chaise à côté du lit, le tapis sous le lit,** etc. It should be possible to get some amusing interior decorating. This drill combines knowledge of spatial relations and directions while encouraging students' sense of humor.

3. Note de grammaire 26: Les adjectifs précédents les noms. Present the following mnemonic aid for remembering adjectives before nouns, which was developed by Constance Knop of the University of Wisconsin at Madison:

B **(Beauty)**	**A** **(Age)**	**G** **(Goodness)**	**S** **(Size)**
beau	jeune	bon	grand
joli	vieux	mauvais	gros
	nouveau	gentil	petit
			long

4. Note de grammaire 27: Le verbe *prendre*. Introduce this verb by taking a book and saying: **Je prends ce livre.** Then ask the question: **Est-ce que je prends ce livre?** Answer: **Oui, je prends ce livre.** Then give the book to a student: **Prends ce livre!** After repeating this routine several times, present the verb formally.

Students may also act out dramatic renditions of the following verbs, using the Wave format described in **Chapitre 2,** Step 16: **apprendre, comprendre, surprendre, prendre, reprendre.** Student 1 mimes and uses **apprendre** in a sentence, Student 2 repeats the mime and then adds his/her own sentence, and so on, until the last student in the group, who must present all five sentences as a dramatic presentation. In these early rounds, when this activity is performed in class, it's best that you create and orchestrate the scenario.

5. Note de grammaire 28: Changements orthographiques. As homework, have students create sentences using the ten target verbs. In class, assign teams of five students to use the Wave format to act out five target verbs.

6. Note de grammaire 29: Les pronoms d'objet direct. This is a difficult concept for American students, but if you hold the explanation to the few rules listed in the text, the problems should be minimized. The difficulty lies not in comprehension but in breaking old habits. Therefore we have devoted many drills to this topic. To clarify, stress the directness of the link between verb and object—for instance: **Je vois le garçon.** Point out that the progression moves immediately from verb to object—that is, there are no interfering words.

7. Note de grammaire 30: Les verbes *pouvoir, vouloir* et *savoir*. Point out the similarities that appear in the conjugations. I also introduce the proverbs **Savoir c'est pouvoir** and **Vouloir c'est pouvoir**. Students take note of the grammatical structure and employ these expressions on many occasions.

8. Travaux pratiques. Although most questions continue to be asked in the **vous** form, the questions students ask of classmates utilize the **tu** form to reflect the more likely form of address among young people and to provide broader practice.

9. Micrologue. This **Micrologue** introduces Voltaire. It may be presented as a brief reading passage or in the speed-writing format described in **Chapitre 2,** Step 13.

10. Lecture. The reading gives some common-sense advice to students who plan to visit any foreign country. Its goal is to demystify cultural shock by exploring the three students' belief that they were harshly treated by the taxi driver and by the clerk at the railroad station and explaining that these are in fact normal occurrences among people anywhere.

The **Lectures** may be treated in class or assigned as homework. When the passages are done as homework, students may also be asked to read lines or paragraphs aloud in class for correction. At the end of each passage, they should be asked to restate in their own words the gist of what they've read.

This reading provides an excellent opportunity to compare American cab drivers with French **chauffeurs de taxi**.

11. Coup d'œil. To check students' grasp of chapter contents, ask them to create new examples for each point in the **Coup d'œil.**

Chapitre 7: Le déjeuner

1. Vocabulaire illustré. Because food is the topic of this chapter's vocabulary, this would be a good time to construct a **Micrologue** based on a recipe for a French dish. Supplementary vocabulary may include **un céleri, un chou-fleur, un chou brocoli; une framboise, un kiwi.**

Since Robert has his first meal in France in this chapter, it may be well to point out various customs observed by the French at mealtime. Both hands, but not elbows, should always be visible on the table. The French hold their eating utensils in a different way from Americans:

the fork is held in the left hand and is used for eating food, while the right hand holds the knife. Lettuce is not cut with a knife, but is folded in small portions with a fork. Fruit is held with a fork, peeled with a knife, and eaten with a fork. One lays both the knife and fork across the plate when finished with the meal.

2. Note de grammaire 31: L'article partitif. To emphasize the meaning of the partitive, bring in some of the items shown in the **Vocabulaire illustré.** For instance, say **"J'aime bien les légumes"** and point to a number of vegetables. Then say **"On fait une soupe à l'oignon en employant des oignons"** while pointing to a few onions. Students will thus see that you are using only some onions. Continue using other foods to reinforce the point.

3. Note de grammaire 32: Il est/C'est. Stress that any modified noun takes **c'est** + **un** or **une** to translate *he* or *she is*: **C'est une bonne actrice,** but **Elle est actrice.**

4. Note de grammaire 33: Le passé composé avec *avoir*. The **passé composé** is troublesome for students because they must remember which auxiliary verb to use. The problem can be minimized if verbs that take **avoir** are thoroughly taught first. Students have already learned an adequate number of such verbs to practice with. A great number of drills are thus devoted to mastering the **passé composé.**

When the drills have been performed, start a story using the present, the near future, and the **passé composé,** calling out the tense that you want in each instance and designating a respondent by tossing a ball as described in **Chapitre 3,** Step 10. Or using any of the preceding **Scénarios,** ask students to change all appropriate verb forms to the **passé composé.**

5. Note de grammaire 34: Pronoms d'objet direct et le passé composé. By this time, students should have grasped the basics of replacing a direct object noun by a direct object pronoun. Now, concentrate on showing them that agreement occurs only when a direct object precedes a verb in the **passé composé** formed with **avoir.**

6. Note de grammaire 35: Le verbe *boire*. With the verb **boire** we have completed the vocabulary required for communication well above survival level. I point this out to my classes to highlight the progress they are making.

7. Travaux pratiques. The Prévert poem is another short drama which highlights use of agreement and the **passé composé.**

8. Micrologue. This discussion of Nicole's breakfast allows you to assign a comparative exercise on breakfast in France and the United States.

9. Création et récréation. In this instance, Monique's story may also be a comparative cultural exercise.

10. Vocabulaire. Reinforce the extensive vocabulary in this chapter by writing the following table of words on the chalkboard and asking students to eliminate the term that does not belong to the group. To generate a good discussion, ask them to explain their choices.

	A	B	C	D	E
1.	monter	mourir	sauter	descendre	tomber
2.	boisson	bière	pâté	vin blanc	vin rouge
3.	agneau	poulet	veau	bœuf	porc
4.	baguette	croissant	éclair	pain	mousse au chocolat
5.	artichaut	asperge	carotte	fraise	aubergine
6.	cerise	banane	oignon	poire	pomme

Students should eliminate 1 C, 2 C, 3 B, 4 E, 5 D, 6 C.

11. Bring in pictures or the actual foods listed in the vocabulary and place them in several piles on a table at one end of the room. Give four or five students each a different list of items to gather. For instance, one list may contain pepper, potatoes, butter, eggplant, and mustard, while another list may contain salt, sugar, bread, onions, and asparagus. See who can be the first to bring you the objects on the list.

12. Coup d'œil. It is advisable to allocate a full class to this review section from time to time.

Chapitre 8: Robert s'installe

1. Vocabulaire illustré. Given that the **Vocabulaire illustré** deals with clothing, you may have students organize a fashion show. Another technique is to have four students stand in front of the class and to describe one person's clothing until the class guesses whom you have in mind. Pause after every fifteen seconds of your description until the class identifies the person.

2. Note de grammaire 36: Position des adjectifs. Remind students that adjectives that follow the noun are usually longer than those that precede the noun, except for the colors.

3. Note de grammaire 37: Le féminin des adjectifs. Emphasize the proper pronunciation and spelling of each adjective.

4. Note de grammaire 38: Les verbes réguliers en *-re*. This is the third and last group of regular verbs. Again, given the fact that the rules for forming the present indicative are not difficult (and assuming some degree of control of the preceding two classes), students should appreciate the fact that **vendre** represents the last of the regular verb groups. Students may be told that they are now capable of conjugating any regular verb in French in the tenses presented thus far.

5. Note de grammaire 39: Le verbe *dormir*. The similarities among the verbs like **dormir** enable students to grasp them rather quickly. Because the **passé composé** with **être** will not be taught until the next grammar note, avoid using **partir** and **sortir** in the **passé composé.**

6. Note de grammaire 40: Le passé composé avec *être*. Draw the closest possible association with these verbs and the house of Mme Etre. It is a useful mnemonic device.

Verbs which may take either **avoir** or **être** may be demonstrated rather easily. For instance, leave the room, saying: **Je sors de la salle de classe.** For contrast, you might sneeze and then act out and say: **Je sors un mouchoir de ma poche.** Then put both sentences in the **passé composé** with the appropriate auxiliary verbs. Remember that there are only five such verbs, in addition to **sortir,** which take **avoir** with a direct object: **descendre: J'ai descendu la rue. / monter: Il a monté les valises. / passer: Elle a passé trois semaines à Paris. / (r)entrer: J'ai rentré la voiture dans le garage. / retourner: On a retourné la crêpe.**

7. Micrologue. This **Micrologue** reflects style at two moments of French history. Are there comparisons to be made in our society?

8. Lecture. The questions that deal with the reading on French customs could generate interesting insights into American habits.

9. Coup d'œil. Question students on the points raised in the review. Have they been doing their own self-evaluations? Do the quiz and test results prove that they are conscientiously checking their progress? Do they believe they have worked hard enough at gaining mastery? Take time to conduct a thorough discussion.

10. Vocabulaire. Words that start with the same first two letters are drawn on the board—for instance, **la cheminée, le chapeau, les chaussures, le chemin, le cheval.** A student then recounts a story using each word in the order that you specify. Next, rearrange the words and ask a second student to relate a story using the new sequence.

Chapitre 9: La mobylette

1. Since mopeds are now fairly common in the United States, students may enjoy learning the following (optional) vocabulary: **le guidon** *handlebars,* **le rétroviseur** *rearview mirror,* **le frein** *brake,* **la selle** *seat,* **le phare** *headlight,* **la pompe** *pump,* **la poche à outils** *tool kit,* **la chaîne** *chain,* **la pédale** *pedal,* **le pneu** *tire.*

2. Note de grammaire 41: Les pronoms compléments d'objet indirect. Here I point out the indirect transmission of the verb's action to the object. On the chalkboard I draw a broken arrow to show that the transmission of the action is indirect:

Je parle à l'homme.

I then contrast this with an example of a direct object:

Je vois le garçon.

I then introduce the indirect object pronouns and reinforce them by having students use other verbs that take indirect objects, such as **répondre** and **téléphoner,** in full sentences.

3. Note de grammaire 42: *Y* et *en*. Have students create their own scenario along the lines of Inspector Klutzo's adventure. As a cue, draw a donkey on the board and write over its head **Y EN!**

4. Note de grammaire 43: Les nombres ordinaux. For further practice of ordinal numbers, bring in pictures of presidents of the United States and have students identify them—for example: **Le premier président des Etats-Unis s'appelle Washington.** To jog students' memories, label each president's picture with a cardinal number indicating his term.

5. Note de grammaire 44: Les verbes pronominaux. This is probably the most difficult construction for an American student to master. We have tried to simplify it as much as possible and have provided an abundance of drills to reinforce each usage. I introduce the pronominal verbs with this definition of marriage **(se marier)** by Hippolyte Taine:

On s'étudie trois semaines,
On s'aime trois mois,
On se dispute trois ans,
On se tolère trente ans.

A more modern version might go like this:

On s'entend bien,
On s'embrasse,
On se marie,
On est heureux,
Ou on divorce.

Note that **divorcer** is not reflexive.

Reinforce the use of the pronominal verbs by designating students to use the Wave to dramatize the following pronominal verbs: **se réveiller, se laver, se brosser les dents, s'habiller, se dépêcher.**

Given that the verb **s'asseoir** has already appeared in the imperative form **asseyez-vous!,** you may want to introduce the full conjugation at this time.

6. Note de grammaire 45: Le passé composé des verbes pronominaux. Stress that in most cases the past participle of a pronominal verb agrees with the reflexive pronoun. Once students have grasped the general rules of agreement between subjects and objects and past participles, the rules of agreement for pronominal verbs should be relatively easy to learn.

Remind students of the rules of agreement between past participles and subjects or objects. Remind students that with the verb **avoir** there is agreement only if the direct object precedes the verb.

7. Micrologue. This **Micrologue** is on the **Quartier latin.** Parallels may be formed with the student quarter of your city or with the student center on your campus.

8. Coup d'œil. I cannot overstate the importance of having students undertake their own diagnostic study of their knowledge at the end of each chapter.

Chapitre 10: Devant la cathédrale

1. A thorough review of the lexical items in previous lessons (for instance, spatial relations, directions, buildings, and road signs) can be practiced using a model village made by the students. As they create such a village on a table top, they would identify the various buildings and install and name streets—ideally, after famous French writers. They could also use toy automobiles to drive to various locations as one student calls out directions.

2. Vocabulaire illustré. Students may practice going from country to country, adding any appropriate comment: **Je vais en Grèce. Il fait beau en Grèce.** For further practice of geographical terms, the reading **"La France géopolitique"** in **Le monde francophone,** at the end of the textbook, may be assigned for at-home reading and class discussion.

3. Note de grammaire 46: Emploi du présent avec *depuis* et *il y a*. The use of **depuis/il y a** requires extensive practice. Students should be reminded that at this point the only possible way to render this construction is in the present tense.

4. Note de grammaire 47: Le futur. Once students have grasped formation of the future tense, drill it thoroughly through the story-telling technique introduced in **Chapitre 3,** Step 10: you call out the tenses you want as a ball is tossed from student to student. Remember to switch tenses appropriately throughout the drill—for instance, start with the present, then go to the **passé composé** and finally the future.

5. Note de grammaire 48: Les prépositions avec les noms de lieux. Building on what was started with the **Vocabulaire illustré,** name a country and ask students to identify its capital and state a pertinent fact or two about it. For example: **Je vais en Grèce. Je vais rester à Athènes et je vais y étudier le grec. Il fait beau en Grèce.** Or one might say: **Je viens d'Italie. J'ai appris l'italien à Rome...**

6. Note de grammaire 49: L'infinitif après une préposition. Emphasize that after conjugated verb + *preposition*, French always uses an infinitive, even though the equivalent English verb form may end in *-ing*. The sole exceptions occur after the prepositions **en** and **après.**

7. Note de grammaire 50: Les verbes *dire, lire* et *conduire*. Point out the many similarities between these verbs. Another verb you may add to this group is **traduire.** Stress the differences in the meanings of **parler, dire,** and **raconter:**

Je parle souvent sans penser.	*I often **speak** without thinking.*
Je dis que tu as raison.	***I say** that you are right.*
Elle aime raconter des histoires.	***She likes to tell** stories.*

8. Lecture. This is the final discussion about adjustment to France and French society. Note the emphasis on sensitivity, which is probably the best lesson we can give our students. The passages on adaptation all stress the true key to understanding: there are many differences among people, but there are also many similarities.

9. Création et récréation. Exercise A uses a teaching aid I call an "Ideogram." Its basic purpose is to discourage or eliminate students' visualization of words in English before they say them in French. You can easily adapt this technique to other French structures you'd like to practice, changing the tenses as you proceed through the text.

10. Monique's visit should be based on a local church, temple, or synagogue.

Chapitre 11: L'accident

1. Note de grammaire 51: Le partitif *de*. The three cases when the partitives **du, de la, de l', des** become **de** are featured in this note. It may be helpful to tell students that when the quantity is qualified, the partitive becomes **de: J'ai beaucoup d'argent. / J'ai un bouquet de fleurs.**

2. Note de grammaire 52: Autres expressions négatives. Point out that the second element of each of these negative expressions is readily recognized as having a "positive" meaning: **pas** = *step* (the original sense probably being that one would not yield a step); **jamais** = *ever*; **rien** (from the Latin *rem*) = *thing;* **plus** = *more.*

3. Note de grammaire 53: Le verbe *connaître*. Have students create pairs of sentences that contrast the meanings of **connaître** and **savoir: Je sais la vérité. / Je connais la ville de New York.** Point out that both verbs have idiomatic meanings in the **passé composé:**

Nous avons su qu'elle était là.	***We learned** that she was there.*
J'ai connu Robert à Bourges.	***I met** Robert in Bourges.*
Robert et Nicole se sont connus en France.	***Robert and Nicole met** in France.*

Paraître also means *to look* or *to seem:* **Il paraît fatigué.** Another verb like **paraître** is **disparaître: La lune a disparu derrière les nuages.**

4. Note de grammaire 54: Les pronoms personnels toniques. The old joke about the commander who wanted men to volunteer for pleasant duty in France might be stated here:

COMMANDANT: Et pour ce service agréable je désire des soldats volontaires qui parlent français. Qui veut offrir ses services?
SOLDAT: Je.

Once students understand disjunctive pronouns, they should recognize that the soldier's enthusiasm to perform this service was far greater than his knowledge of French.

5. Note de grammaire 55: L'adjectif *quel*. Because this is not a difficult structure, students grasp it relatively quickly.

6. Micrologue. Use this **Micrologue** as a springboard for discussion of differences in French and American pharmacies.

7. Lecture. This is a provocative reading that could lead to amusing comparisons between French and American drivers.

Chapitre 12: En famille

1. Note de grammaire 56: Le verbe *mettre*. Stress the **t** sound in the third person plural form that does not occur in the third person singular. You may also point out that **permettre** and **promettre** take **de** before an infinitive: **Je promets de le faire.** Add that they take **à** before a person: **Elle permet à ses enfants d'y aller.**

2. Note de grammaire 57: Position des pronoms compléments d'objet. Remind students that they have already learned how the position of object pronouns in French differs from English usage. Now they need merely remember that when two object pronouns are used, direct object pronouns precede indirect object pronouns and that first and second person pronouns precede third person pronouns.

3. Note de grammaire 58: Les pronoms compléments avec l'impératif. Point out the similarities between the position of object pronouns in both French and English imperatives.

4. Note de grammaire 59: Les adverbes. A review of adjectives will lay a firm foundation for learning the formation of adverbs.

5. Note de grammaire 60: Le verbe *envoyer*. Along with thorough practice of **envoyer** and **payer,** review verbs with other orthographic changes. Also ask: **Combien avez-vous payé votre pull? vos chaussures? votre jupe?**

6. Lecture. Ionesco's *La Cantatrice chauve* scores a direct hit on our tendency to talk, talk, talk without listening to others' responses and on our ability to tune out messages we don't want to hear. Words ricochet back and forth like a ping-pong match gone wild with no one keeping score.

7. Création et récréation. Use the chapter-opening illustrations for review by assigning a different picture to each of several students and having them describe the events. This may be done extemporaneously.

Chapitre 13: Une lettre: choses à écrire

1. Coin culturel. Have students contrast the roles of women in American and French societies.

2. Note de grammaire 61: L'imparfait. Emphasize that the same stems and endings are used to form the imperfect tense of both regular and irregular verbs, with the exception of **être.** To reinforce the notion of simultaneous, ongoing action in the past, have three students stand before the class. They will act out and construct sentences using pairs of infinitives suggested by their classmates. For example, for the verbs **danser** and **chanter,** Student 3 says **pendant que,** while Student 1 dances and Student 2 sings. Student 3 then states the full sentence: **Numéro 1 dansait pendant que Numéro 2 chantait.**

3. Note de grammaire 62: L'imparfait ou le passé composé? To demonstrate the notion of interrupted versus ongoing action, once again have three students act out and construct sentences using pairs of infinitives suggested by the class, but this time give Student 3 a choice between two cues: **pendant que** and **quand.** Thus, in this case, if the infinitives are **téléphoner** and **frapper** and Student 3 gives the cue **quand,** Student 1 talks on the phone when Student 2 knocks on the door. Student 3 then narrates: **Numéro 1 téléphonait à son ami quand Numéro 2 a frappé à la porte.** To emphasize the difference between the imperfect and the **passé composé,** the action in the **passé composé** should be performed quickly.

4. Note de grammaire 63: Le comparatif et le superlatif des adjectifs. Practice these forms by having students compare the height of one classmate to another.

5. Note de grammaire 64: Le comparatif et le superlatif des adverbes et des quantités. Again, students can make comparisons among their classmates: **Qui parle vite? Qui parle le plus vite de la classe?** Etc.

6. Note de grammaire 65: Le verbe *écrire*. As in the past, dramatize the verb as you introduce it. In this case, as students are writing an assignment in class, write something on the board (say, the verb **écrire**) and announce: **J'écris.** Turn to a student and say: **Tu écris,** etc. Once you have presented all forms informally, present the verb formally.

7. Micrologue. Ask the class if there is an institution comparable to the **Académie française** in the United States. Should there be? Should a U.S. government agency control what is and what is not acceptable in English?

8. Lecture. These two letters demonstrate the epistolary art form cultivated by the French.

9. Création et récréation. As always, these activities should be fully exploited. Insist on the proper beginnings and endings of letters.

10. Coup d'œil. Appoint a student to lead the review and answer any questions his/her classmates may have.

Chapitre 14: A l'hôtel

1. Note de grammaire 66: Les pronoms relatifs *qui, que* et *où*. If students do not understand the grammatical terminology in the grammar note, have them consult the **Glossary of Grammatical Terms** in the appendices of the textbook. Once they understand the basic terminology, it will be easier for them to understand the relationships we are trying to establish.

2. Note de grammaire 67: Les pronoms relatifs *dont* et *à qui*. You may find it helpful to present a summary chart of the relative pronouns at this time:

	ANTECEDENT	RELATIVE CLAUSE	
SUBJECT (**QUI**)	La femme	**qui** est là	est la directrice.
DIRECT OBJECT (**QUE**)	La femme	**que** vous voyez	est la directrice.
OBJECT OF **DE** (**DONT**)	La femme	**dont** vous parlez	est la directrice.
OBJECTS OF OTHER	La femme	**sur qui** vous comptez	est la directrice.
PREPOSITIONS (**QUI**)	La femme	**avec qui** vous travaillez	est la directrice.

3. Note de grammaire 68: Le pronom relatif *lequel*. This relative pronoun could be added to the above chart, stressing the fact that it is most often used to refer to things or animals and that it is always preceded by a preposition.

4. Note de grammaire 69: *Tout* et autres expressions indéfinies de quantité. Indefinite articles should pose no problem since much has already been said about the functioning of adjectives.

5. Note de grammaire 70: Les verbes *vivre* et *suivre*. Point out the similarities in the conjugations of these verbs, as well as their resemblance to **écrire.** When you introduce **vivre,** make an animated gesture to show life. To introduce **suivre,** draw one stick figure following another. The more we deal with direct images, the faster students will acquire the verbs. Dramatization is always appropriate.

6. Micrologue. Because this **Micrologue** describes a French professor, it is a good springboard for student descriptions of an American professor and comparisons of the two. Having students describe your day and your conduct, as they perceive them, can be an amusing assignment for all concerned.

7. Lecture. Students often show great interest in the French educational system. Point out that the French prize education highly and that status is determined by one's educational background. Encourage them to make many comparisons with our own school system. Which system seems more interesting? More demanding? etc.

8. Coup d'œil. This **Coup d'œil** may be run as a quiz show, with one student serving as the quiz master and two teams giving examples of each grammatical point presented. A team scores one point for each correct example offered.

Chapitre 15: Une coïncidence!

1. Note de grammaire 71: Les pronoms interrogatifs *qui* et *que*. Emphasize the use of the **est-ce que** to avoid inversion with interrogative pronouns.

2. **Note de grammaire 72: Les prépositions avec les pronoms interrogatifs.** Stress the close similarities to English usage here. To have some fun with practicing **qu'est-ce que** and **qu'est-ce que c'est que,** ask students for definitions of such terms as **le mariage, le bonheur, un chauffeur de taxi, un professeur, un étudiant.**

3. **Note de grammaire 73: Le pronom interrogatif *lequel*.** After the presentation of **lequel,** offer students a choice of several objects and use **lequel** to ask them to state their preferences.

4. **Note de grammaire 74: Quantités approximatives.** Remind students that not every number can be converted into an approximation by adding **-aine.**

5. **Note de grammaire 75: Négations: type ne... que.** Contrast negative expressions like **ne... que** with the negative expressions like **ne... pas** introduced earlier.

6. **Lecture.** To supplement this reading on newspapers in France, bring in different French newspapers for students to read in class, or assign such reading as homework. Contrasts should be drawn with American newspapers.

7. **Création et récréation.** Stage a press conference with an important person, living or dead, real or imagined. This exercise is eagerly performed by students. If you play the role of the interviewee (or if one of your colleagues assumes this role), you can work in more cultural themes. It would be possible, for instance, to interview Napoleon, or Louis XIV, or any other historical personage. Students are given simple instructions: Any questions may be asked, but they should be kept short and humorous, if possible. Students should write down all answers and create an article on the interview as homework. You may ask them to write the article as an interview, quoting only what was said, or you may prefer to have them use the journalistic who? why? when? where? what? You may require that the articles be written in direct or indirect discourse.

Chapitre 16: Métiers

1. **Allons plus loin.** Take this opportunity to ask questions such as: **Qu'est-ce que l'avocat a étudié? le comptable? l'infirmière?** etc.

2. **Note de grammaire 76: Le conditionnel.** Call attention to the obvious similarities between the imperfect endings and the conditional endings.

3. **Note de grammaire 77: *Si* (hypothèse + condition).** It is important to emphasize the relationships between the tenses used in the hypothetical clause and the result, or main, clause so that students will more readily understand the relationships between the past conditional and the pluperfect later.

4. **Travaux pratiques.** Exercise B asks students to write clauses expressing fantasies and results. This technique is always unanimously enjoyed by students. To assure grammatical accuracy, it is best that you read the completed sentences. Then have the corrected responses reproduced and distributed to all.

5. **Note de grammaire 78: Les pronoms démonstratifs.** You can reinforce the use of the demonstrative pronoun by playing a simple game. Without the rest of the class knowing, let one student in on the secret of the game. That student leaves the room while the rest of the class agrees upon an object in the room that he/she must identify. Your student-partner knows that the chosen object will be the one you will designate *after a red object.*

The class will invariably want to know how the student managed to guess the object so quickly, so arrange a second round. This time your student-partner knows that the chosen object will be the next one *after anything that is white.* Follow the same procedures for a third round, only this time the object will be *after anything blue.*

Should the class insist that the object be identified on the very first attempt, tell your student-partner that your words will signal the color. Thus, in the first round you may say *how angry you are* that no one trusts you (anger suggests red); for the second round, say that *you can't remember anything* (a blank suggests white); for the third round, indicate *how sad you are* that no one believes you (sadness suggests a blue mood). A typical round 1 exchange would be:

INSTRUCTOR: Je pense à un objet. Est-ce ce tableau noir-ci?
STUDENT: Non, ce n'est pas celui-là.

INSTRUCTOR: Est-ce cette porte-ci?
STUDENT: Non, ce n'est pas celle-là.
INSTRUCTOR: Est-ce ce livre-ci? *(The book has a red cover.)*
STUDENT: Non, ce n'est pas celui-là.
INSTRUCTOR: Est-ce mur-ci?
STUDENT: Oui, c'est celui-là.

This game may be adapted to other structures as well, so it's best not to reveal its secret to the class.

6. Note de grammaire 79: Pronoms relatifs sans antécédent défini. Because students are familiar with the relative pronouns **qui** and **que,** the addition of **ce** to replace a specific antecedent should not create too many difficulties. The main difference to emphasize here is that **que** becomes **quoi.**

7. Note de grammaire 80: Les verbes *rire* et *courir*. This is a good time to have the class read La Fontaine's **"Le lièvre et la tortue."** The fable is an example of an important literary tradition that is centered around whether it is wise to **courir.**

8. Micrologue. This **Micrologue** introduces the poem in the **Lecture** that follows and is intended to bring out the meaning of the reading. Make sure students know the vocabulary, some of which may be illustrated on the chalkboard.

9. Lecture. This depiction of the plight of a young black child in a school that does not reflect his needs has far-ranging possibilities for discussion. Have the students study the reading for homework. Then have them read it aloud in class and discuss it. The debate suggested on page 420 of the text could precede or follow the general discussion. Note that there are no comprehension questions on the reading itself, since key questions were covered with the preparatory **Micrologue.** Should you want to ask more comprehension questions, the following are suggested:

1. Où l'école se trouve-t-elle?
2. Qu'est-ce que l'enfant veut faire?
3. Où veut-il dormir?
4. Quand veut-il se réveiller?
5. Qu'est-ce qu'on raconte?
6. Qu'est-ce qu'il ne veut pas devenir?
7. Qu'est-ce qu'il préfère écouter?
8. Qu'est-ce que les noirs apprennent dans ces écoles?
9. Qu'est-ce que ne savent pas faire, « ces messieurs de la ville »?

Chapitre 17: Devant le gymnase

1. Sports are featured in the **Coin culturel** and the **Vocabulaire illustré,** allowing for many discussions of favorite sports, famous figures in each category, which country has the best athletes in each category, etc.

2. Note de grammaire 81: Le verbe *falloir*. In practicing this structure the question **Qu'est-ce qu'il vous faut pour être heureux/heureuse?** should elicit interesting responses.

3. Note de grammaire 82: Le subjonctif et son emploi. The simple and automatic usages of the subjunctive are stressed here. Have students express what they believe another should do urgently: **Il faut que...** ; what they should like others to do: **Je veux que...** ; what they doubt others can do: **Je doute que...** ; what emotions they feel when someone does something: **Je suis furieux que...**

4. Note de grammaire 83: Les subjonctifs irréguliers. Most of the irregular verbs students will use in the subjunctive are presented here.

5. Note de grammaire 84: Indicatif ou subjonctif? Stress the differences between subjunctive and indicative and have students make up their own examples of each usage.

6. Note de grammaire 85: Emploi du subjonctif après des conjunctions. Automatic usages.

7. Micrologue. Once again the **Micrologue** is used to introduce the **Lecture** that follows.

8. Lecture. This passage by Léopold Senghor is distinguished by the author's sensitivity.

It also shows what students can expect of an experience in a foreign country if they too are sensitive. Here are some additional questions:

1. Qu'est-ce que M. Senghor a d'abord connu de Paris?
2. Qu'est-ce que les fumées d'usines n'arrivent pas à ternir?
3. Comment la lumière reste-t-elle?
4. Qu'est-ce qu'elle anime?
5. Quel est l'objet de sa quête?
6. Qu'est-ce qu'il a mis dans sa quête?
7. Quel est le sceau de l'esprit de Paris?
8. A quoi est-ce que tout est ramené?

8. Création et récréation. In preparation for this observation exercise, arrange items around the classroom that you would like students to notice (a specific number of chairs in a row, a book or two on a certain chair, a wastepaper basket, a briefcase, a plant, etc.). The goal is to see how many objects students will notice—what they will see, hear, touch—without your prompting. When students arrive, tell them to follow you through the classroom and to remain silent and alert throughout the walk. Give no further instructions. At the end of the walk, when students have returned to their seats, write three categories on the chalkboard—**Choses vues, Choses entendues, Choses touchées**—and ask students to complete each list to the best of their recollection. Then compare results.

The goal of this activity is twofold: it helps review vocabulary and, more significantly, it underscores the importance of being alert to all that occurs around oneself. Class discussion may center on the needs to be open to one's surroundings and to realize how many things may escape notice. These topics may be related to the readings about life in France and lead to the conclusion that students should approach each new experience with an open mind and seek out the full picture rather than leap to hasty judgments.

Chapitre 18: Au cinéma

1. The cinema and theater are featured in the **Coin culturel** and the **Vocabulaire illustré,** allowing for many discussions of favorite movies, plays, actors/actresses, etc. Have teams of students make up publicity for current movies.

2. **Note de grammaire 86: Récapitulation du subjonctif.** Review the use of the subjunctive.

3. **Note de grammaire 87: Le verbe *devoir*.** Have the students write sentences demonstrating the nuances in meaning of the verb **devoir.**

4. **Note de grammaire 88: Les verbes *recevoir* et *pleuvoir*.** Models of usage.

5. **Note de grammaire 89: Emplois de l'infinitif.** Students should be able to use each structure correctly within the context of drills. Tell students that keeping in mind **être ou ne pas être** will steer them clear of many problems. Continue the pattern with **manger ou ne pas manger** and **fumer ou ne pas fumer** and let them come up with many more similar examples. Remind students that the past infinitive should be used after the preposition **après.**

6. **Note de grammaire 90: Le participe présent.** This part of speech is acquired with relative ease. Point out that students have been using participles as adjectives **(charmant)** since early in the text.

7. Now is an appropriate time to have students write and prepare skits for performance or videotaping. One approach is for them to choose lines from the **Scénarios** to tell their own stories, create a soap opera, or write a detective story. (This chapter's **Lecture** presents a sample detective story.) When they are through with their copy, correct it but do not rewrite it. The play should be theirs: they should write it in teams of their own choosing, rehearse it, and stage it. The skits should be presented around the end of **Chapitre 19.**

8. **Lecture.** This passage from Maigret is typical of Simenon's many stories. The descriptions are vivid, the language simple, the characters realistic, the plot gripping.

Chapitre 19: Les villages

1. **Minitel** and the post office are featured in the **Coin culturel** and the **Vocabulaire illustré.** They contain practical information for communicating by **Minitel,** telephone, telegram, and letters. These items can lead to many discussions about systems of communication.

2. **Note de grammaire 91: Les prépositions avec l'infinitif.** Note that **Appendix A** carries a more complete list of verbs and prepositions for instructors who prefer to go into fuller detail.

3. Note de grammaire 92: Le verbe *ouvrir*. Ouvrir and verbs conjugated like it.

4. Note de grammaire 93: Les pronoms possessifs. Make sure that students always show agreement with the object possessed and are careful of contractions with prepositions.

The game suggested in **Chapitre 16,** Step 4, may be adapted for use with the possessive pronouns. A typical round 1 exchange would be:

INSTRUCTOR: Je pense à un objet. Est-ce ce tableau-ci?
STUDENT: Non, ce n'est pas le vôtre.
INSTRUCTOR: Est-ce cette porte-ci?
STUDENT: Non, ce n'est pas la vôtre.
INSTRUCTOR: Est-ce ce livre-ci? *(The book has a red cover.)*
STUDENT: Non, ce n'est pas le vôtre.
INSTRUCTOR: Est-ce mur-ci?
STUDENT: Oui, c'est le vôtre.

5. Note de grammaire 94: Le plus-que-parfait de l'indicatif and **Note de grammaire 95: Le conditionnel passé.** These two tenses should be worked together, as were the imperfect and the conditional. Again, pair off students to write clauses independently—some beginning with **si** and using the pluperfect, and others containing the past conditional (see **Chapitre 16,** Step 4).

6. Micrologue. This **Micrologue** advises students to consider the provinces as a good place to begin to learn about France, rather than to base their opinions on Paris alone. Sound advice.

7. Lecture. By capturing wheat's mystical, almost sacred qualities, Péguy's prose poem highlights the central role this grain plays in French life.

8. Travaux pratiques. Pascal's sublime meditation on **le roseau pensant** dramatically demonstrates the depth of this seventeenth-century French thinker.

9. One way to end the last class is to call upon teams of students to present **Scénarios** without warm-up sessions. For instance, give the title and perhaps the first line or so of a **Scénario** and let the team take over. Their adaptations should be entertaining.

10. The prepared student productions should now be ready for presentation either live or on videotape. Invite as many people as possible to attend, including other sections of the same French course.

Chapitre facultatif: Au bureau de poste/Dîner d'adieu

This chapter is strictly optional. The grammar notes for this chapter appear in the main text, but the **Scénarios** and other material appear only in this *Instructor's Manual.* You may decide to read the **Scénarios** to the students or you may simply summarize their contents. It is also possible to photocopy the dialogues and have students read them on their own.

Scénario

Au bureau de poste

ROBERT: Je serais resté ici bien plus longtemps si j'avais pu, mais maintenant que le stage se termine, je dois envoyer un télégramme aux Etats-Unis.

MME FOURCHET: Pourquoi pas téléphoner?

ROBERT: Parce que je connais ma mère. Elle va me filer une liste de courses à faire dans les boutiques de Charles de Gaulle et je n'ai pas envie de faire cette corvée. Je veux seulement prévenir mes parents de mon heure d'arrivée.

MME FOURCHET: Téléphone tout de même! Ça leur fera plaisir de t'entendre. Ne te gêne pas pour utiliser notre téléphone! Vas-y!

ROBERT: Merci, je préfère envoyer un télégramme. J'irai au bureau de poste. Après tout, ce sera pour moi une expérience de plus.

A la poste, il rencontre Nicole et Henry. Henry est en train d'acheter les derniers timbres sortis pour sa collection.

NICOLE: Tiens, salut! Que fais-tu ici?

ROBERT: Je vais envoyer un télégramme chez moi.

HENRY: Heureusement que tu m'y fais penser, il faut que j'envoie le mien aussi. Quand tu l'auras fait, j'enverrai le mien.

Ils l'accompagnent au guichet.

L'EMPLOYE: ... dix-huit, dix-neuf... vous avez encore droit à trois mots pour le même prix.
ROBERT: « All my best. »
L'EMPLOYE: Qu'est-ce que cela veut dire?
ROBERT: C'est à peu près l'équivalent de: « Veuillez agréer l'expression de mes sentiments les meilleurs ».
L'EMPLOYE: *(avec un ton moqueur)* Veuillez me donner vingt-deux francs!

Henry envoie aussi son télégramme et ils sortent de la poste en riant.

NICOLE: Sérieusement, mes amis, c'est dommage de vous voir partir. Vous avez fait des progrès sensass! Vous avez fait un bon job. C'est un bon show et tous les deux, vous êtes des stars. Vous êtes des super mecs!
HENRY ET ROBERT: Oh, là, là! Quel franglais!
NICOLE: Si, si, c'est vrai. Pour parler français, je dirais que vous êtes vachement bien! Vous allez me manquer.
HENRY: Mais nous ne sommes pas encore tout à fait partis... On va se revoir au dîner d'adieu.

Synonymes et expressions approximatives

stage = période d'études pratiques
me filer ° = me donner
une liste de shopping *(franglais)* = une liste de courses à faire
prévenir = avertir, aviser
ne te gêne pas = ne sois pas timide, ne sois pas aussi réservé
salut = bonjour
vous avez encore droit à = vous pouvez encore avoir
dévisageant = regardant avec insistance
c'est dommage = c'est regrettable
sensass ° = sensationnels, excellents, formidables, extraordinaires
des super mecs ° = des surhommes
vachement ° = très

Questions sur le scénario

1. Maintenant que le stage se termine, qu'est-ce que Robert doit faire?
2. Pourquoi ne téléphone-t-il pas à sa mère?
3. Pour quelles raisons Mme Fourchet insiste-t-elle qu'il téléphone?
4. Qui Robert rencontre-t-il à la poste?
5. Qu'est-ce que Henry fait à la poste?
6. Qu'est-ce que Henry fera?
7. A combien de mots Robert a-t-il encore droit pour le même prix?
8. Que veut dire en français: « All my best »?
9. Pourquoi Nicole pense-t-elle qu'il est dommage que Robert et Henry partent?
10. D'après Nicole, comment parlent-ils français?

Scénario

Dîner d'adieu

Toutes les familles françaises sont réunies à l'Auberge du Vieux Moulin. Elles y sont avec leurs fils et leurs filles américains. Monsieur Galant, le propriétaire, a préparé un repas succulent. On entend la musique d'une chaîne stéréo. Il y a aussi un groupe de danseurs folkloriques qui, avec leur musique et leurs danses, régaleront la compagnie plus tard.

LE PROFESSEUR: *(continuant son discours de remerciement)*... et sans vous, nos pères et nos mères français, notre séjour aurait été simplement académique. Grâce à vous, nous avons habité dans vos foyers et partagé votre vie; vous nous avez accueillis chaleureusement. Si nous n'avions pas été hébergés par vous, nous n'aurions jamais connu la base de la culture française. Malgré la brièveté de notre séjour, nous nous sentons très proches des Français et emportons avec nous d'excellents souvenirs d'amitié qui ont créé des liens très forts entre nous.

ROBERT: Vous voyez, madame, c'est exactement ce que je ressens. Je cherchais mes mots pour vous dire la même chose.

MME FOURCHET: Nous gardons aussi un excellent souvenir de ton séjour. Combien de fromages as-tu goûtés chez nous? Tu t'en souviens?

ROBERT: Exactement soixante-six, ou un par jour.

MME FOURCHET: Alors il faudra que tu reviennes pour goûter les deux cent soixante-quatorze qui restent! Et en échange tu nous feras goûter la cuisine américaine. En attendant, mettons-nous à table et profitons de la bonne chère.

Marguerite, Henry et Robert se retrouvent en aparté avant de passer à table.

HENRY: Ecoutez, chers amis, portons un toast à nos progrès en français! Nous avons tenu notre promesse, nous n'avons jamais parlé anglais ensemble et notre français est digne de...

MARGUERITE: ... digne de tous ceux qui le parlent dans le monde entier. A votre santé!

MARGUERITE, HENRY ET ROBERT: A la nôtre! A notre prochaine visite en France!

A la fin de la soirée, tous se sont embrassés et on pouvait entendre la salle résonner de beaucoup de « au revoir » pleins de nostalgie et de promesses de s'écrire souvent.

Synonymes et expressions approximatives

succulent = délicieux, exquis, savoureux, agréable
un tourne-disque = un électrophone, un hi-fi
régaleront = amuseront, distrairont, divertiront
vos foyers = vos maisons, vos familles
accuellis = reçus
chaleureusement = chaudement, avec enthousiasme
proches = près
je ressens = je sens avec émotion ou avec un sentiment agréable
de la bonne chère = du bon repas, des bons mets, des bons plats
en aparté = échangeant des paroles dans un petit groupe séparé

Questions sur le scénario

1. Où les familles sont-elles réunies?
2. Qu'est-ce que M. Galant a préparé?
3. Qu'est-ce qu'on entend?
4. Que feront les danseurs folkloriques?
5. Sans les parents français, qu'aurait été le séjour des Américains?
6. Qu'est-ce que les Français ont fait?
7. Quels sentiments ont les Américains après leur stage?
8. Que demande Mme Fourchet à Robert?
9. Combien de fromages lui propose-t-elle de goûter encore?
10. Pourquoi désire-t-elle se mettre à table?
11. Les trois amis ont-ils tenu leur promesse?
12. Que pensent-ils de leur français?

13. Quel toast portent-ils?
14. Comment la soirée se termine-t-elle?

Exercices de grammaire

The following exercises supplement the **Notes de grammaire** that appear in the main text. These exercises do not appear in the *Student Workbook/Laboratory Manual.*

Note de grammaire A: Le subjonctif passé

Simples substitutions

A.

1. Elle est heureuse *que tu l'aies fait. (que tu sois venu, que vous l'ayez fini, que nous l'ayons choisi, qu'ils l'aient cru, qu'on soit rentré)*
2. Je voudrais *qu'il le fasse. (qu'on le sache, qu'ils puissent le faire, que vous l'étudiiez, qu'elle la conduise, que tu le boives)*
3. J'ai regretté *que vous l'ayez dit. (que vous soyez parti, que tu l'aies dit, qu'il l'ait lu, que nous l'ayons battu, qu'on ait ri à ce moment-là)*

Exercices de transformation

B. Modèle: Je suis content que tu ailles au cinéma aujourd'hui.
Je suis content que tu sois allé au cinéma hier.

1. C'est dommage qu'il ne vienne pas aujourd'hui.
2. Elle doutait que tu écrives pour l'inviter aujourd'hui.
3. Je ne crois pas qu'elle fasse son travail aujourd'hui.
4. Je regrette que tu ne le dises pas aujourd'hui.

C. Modèle: Je suis heureux que vous ayez invité Nicole. *(J'étais heureux)*
J'étais heureux que vous ayez invité Nicole.

1. Elle veut toujours que vous le fassiez. *(Elle voulait)*
2. Nous voudrions bien que vous réussissiez. *(Nous voulons)*
3. Il est possible que nous y allions avec elle. *(Il était possible)*
4. Elle regrette que tu ne l'aies pas accompagnée. *(Elle regrettera)*
5. C'est dommage que nous l'ayons fait. *(C'était dommage)*
6. Je crains que vous ne soyez déçus. *(Je craignais)*

Travaux pratiques

Ecrivez des phrases logiques.

1. il faut/aller/école/demain
2. je doute/conduire/vite
3. il est content/venir/parler/camarades
4. elle veut/vous/faire/repas/demain

Note de grammaire B: Le verbe *plaire*

Simples substitutions

A.

1. *Ce dîner* me plaît. *(Ce taxi, Ce scénario, Ce violon, Ce trombone, Ce poulet)*
2. Tu plais *à mes parents. (à mes amis, à mes frères, à mes sœurs, à mes grands-parents, à mes professeurs, à mes camarades)*
3. Il me déplairait *de balayer la cuisine. (de passer l'aspirateur sur le tapis, de cirer le parquet, de faire la vaisselle, de nettoyer les rideaux, de laver les fenêtres)*

4. *Ni les asperges ni les tomates* ne lui ont plu. *(Ni les croissants ni le pain, Ni les haricots ni les pommes frites, Ni les cerises ni les fraises, Ni les bananes ni les pommes, Ni les aubergines ni les carottes, Ni les oignons ni les petits pois)*

Exercice de transformation

B. Modèle: *Ils* s'y plairont. *(Nous)*
Nous nous y plairons.

1. *Ils* s'y plairont. *(Nous, Il, Vous, Je, Tu)*
2. *Mme Fourchet* s'y plaisait quand il faisait beau. *(Les enfants, Nous, Vous, Je, Tu)*
3. *Je* me tairais s'il le fallait. *(Nous, Elle, Tu, Vous, Elles)*
4. *Il* s'est enfin tu. *(Nous, Je, Vous, Tu, Les chats)*

Travaux pratiques

A. *Respond to each sentence using* **plaire, déplaire,** *or* **se taire.**

Modèle: Je veux manger encore du gigot.
Le gigot me plaît.

1. Hélène voudrait visiter le Québec.
2. Ce film va dégoûter Pierre.
3. Le professeur dira aux étudiants de ne pas faire trop de bruit.
4. Alice n'a pas pu manger les haricots.
5. Elle était heureuse sur la plage quand il faisait beau.
6. La biologie n'est pas mon sujet favori.
7. Dans le temps, Henry aimait la psychologie.
8. Nous aimerions aller au cinéma.

B. *Answer each question using* **plaire, déplaire,** *or* **se taire** *in the appropriate tenses.*

Modèle: Est-ce qu'il vous déplaît de faire vos devoirs?
Oui, il me déplaît de les faire. Je préfère manger de la pizza.

1. Est-ce qu'il vous plaîrait au cinéma d'entendre bavarder les gens? Que leur diriez-vous?
2. Quand vous voulez dormir, vous plaît-il d'entendre la musique excessivement fort? Qu'avez-vous envie de faire?
3. Vous plaîrait-il d'étudier l'astronomie? Pourquoi?
4. Vous tairiez-vous si vous n'étiez pas d'accord avec un prof?
5. Quelle est l'habitude qui vous déplaît le plus?

Note de grammaire C: Le passé simple

Students must be able to identify the **passé simple** because it is important for reading literature. However, because its use in spoken French is negligible, students need not be able to produce this tense themselves. If you find that the exercises below do not provide enough practice, use short literary passages and have students transfer the **passé simple** to the **passé composé.** Here is a sample from Diderot's *La Religieuse:*

> A l'approche de sa mort, elle *se fit* habiller, elle était étendue sur son lit: on lui *administra* les derniers sacrements; elle tenait un Christ entre ses bras. C'était la nuit; les lueurs des flambeaux éclairaient cette scène lugubre. Nous l'entourions, nous fondions en larmes, sa cellule retentissait de cris, lorsque tout à coup ses yeux *brillèrent*, elle *se releva* brusquement, *elle parla;* sa voix était presque aussi forte que dans l'état de santé; le don qu'elle avait perdu lui *revint:* elle nous *reprocha* des larmes que semblaient lui envier un bonheur éternel...

The preceding passage contrasts the use of the imperfect and the **passé simple.** Students should be able to understand it, with the exception of the following words:

les lueurs des flambeaux *the torchlights*
éclairait *illuminated*
lugubre *gloomy*
entourions *surrounded*
fondions *melted*
sa cellule retentissait *her cell (room) echoed*
reprocha *reproached, begrudged*

Exercices de transformation

A. Modèle: Il naquit en Grèce en 1880.
Il est né en Grèce en 1880.

1. Il étudia dans les écoles du pays.
2. Tu finis tes études à l'âge de quinze ans.
3. Nous travaillâmes un peu partout.
4. Ils partirent pour les Etats-Unis en 1896.
5. Vous écrivîtes le livre.
6. Elles tombèrent malade.
7. Elles eurent beaucoup de patience.
8. Il mourut aux Etats-Unis en 1944.

B. Modèle: Ils y allèrent courageusement.
Ils y sont allés courageusement.

1. Nous vînmes tôt.
2. Tu ne voulus jamais nous accompagner.
3. Conduisit-il prudemment?
4. Nous trouvâmes du monde chez vous.
5. Vous partîtes avant la fin de la séance.

Travaux pratiques

Lisez en mettant les passés simples aux passés composés.

1. Elle rencontra Candide et rougit aussi: elle lui dit bonjour..., et Candide lui parla sans savoir ce qu'il disait.
2. En dépit de l'adversité des temps qu'il connut, le paysan accepta le combat parce qu'il aimait la terre. Son travail lui plaisait et le blé était le but *(goal)* de son travail.
3. Je ne pus vous en dire davantage; Mlle de Fare pleurait aussi en m'embrassant, et ce fut en cet état que la surprit la femme de chambre dont je vous ai parlé...
4. Nous dinâmes donc; ce fut lui qui me servit le plus souvent; il but à ma santé...
5. [Maigret] se gratta la tête, choisit deux pipes qu'il glissa *(slipped)* dans sa poche, entrebaîlla *(opened slightly)* la porte du bureau des inspecteurs.
6. [Maigret] endossa son gros pardessus, trouva dans la cour une petite auto de la police et donna l'adresse... Maigret gravit *(went up)* les cinq étages en soupirant *(sighing)*, une porte s'ouvrit sans qu'il ait eu besoin de frapper; Mme Lognon, les yeux et le nez rouges, le fit entrer.

Note de grammaire D: Le futur antérieur

This tense should also be presented for recognition only in the first year.

Simples substitutions

A.

1. *Il l'aura envoyé* quand elle arrivera. *(Tu l'auras fini, On l'aura acheté, Nous l'aurons lu, Ils lui auront téléphoné, Je lui aurai répondu)*
2. *Tu seras sorti* quand je le ferai. *(Elle sera réveillée, Vous serez revenu, Ils seront montés, On sera rentré, Nous serons arrivés)*

Exercices de transformation

B. Une chose avant une autre.

Modèle: Je le ferai quand tu viendras.
Je l'aurai fait quand tu viendras.

1. Vous partirez quand ils arriveront.
2. Nous le lui dirons quand tu seras là.
3. Il le terminera quand elle le verra.
4. Ils mangeront quand nous y entrerons.
5. Elle consultera la liste quand il arrivera.
6. Tu me parleras quand elle téléphonera.
7. Ils monteront quand tu descendras.
8. Tu sortiras quand elle recevra la lettre.
9. Tu arriveras par le train quand il retournera.

C. Modèle: Quand j'aurai lu le livre, je vous le donnerai.
Après avoir lu le livre, je vous le donnerai.

1. Dès que vous l'aurez vu, vous le saurez.
2. Lorsqu'il nous aura retrouvés, il nous le dira.
3. Après que nous serons partis, nous regretterons ce beau pays.
4. Quand nous serons montés, nous y resterons.

Note de grammaire E: La voix passive

Stress the agreement between past participle and subject in this structure.

Simples substitutions

A.
1. Robert est *puni* par le professeur. *(reçu, invité, choisi, aidé, observé)*
2. Brigitte est *aimée* de tous les étudiants. *(admirée, suivie, crainte, détestée, accompagnée)*

Exercices de transformation

B. Modèle: On vendra cette maison dans un mois.
Cette maison sera vendue dans un mois.

1. On invitera ces camarades.
2. On consulte la liste.
3. On époussettera la chambre.
4. On a éteint la lumière.
5. On a perdu son imperméable.

C. Modèle: Cette nouvelle sera annoncée demain.
On annoncera cette nouvelle demain.

1. Le dîner est servi dans l'avion.
2. Il faut que ce vin soit vite bu.
3. Tous ces problèmes ont été discutés.
4. Trois chemises ont été vendues ce matin.
5. Le français est parlé ici.

D. Modèle: Robert a été puni par le professeur.
Le professeur a puni Robert.

1. Cette chemise a été faite par Michelle.
2. La récolte a été détruite par la pluie.
3. Mme Fourchet est flattée par Henry.
4. Robert est observé par le professeur.

E. Modèle: Le professeur surprend les filles.
Les filles sont surprises par le professeur.

1. L'employé a reçu l'argent.
2. Les enfants observeront les moutons.
3. Son collègue a déçu cet homme.
4. Le chauffeur l'humiliera.

F. Modèle: Mme Fourchet était aimée des enfants.
Les enfants aimaient Mme Fourchet.

1. Le professeur était détesté des étudiants.
2. Robert est craint de tous les étudiants.
3. Elle est suivie de tous ses admirateurs.
4. Sa mort a été regrettée de tout le monde.

F. Modèle: Les paysans détestent le mauvais temps.
Le mauvais temps est détesté des paysans.

1. Les chats craignent les chiens.
2. Tous les étudiants accompagnent Brigitte.
3. Tous les disciples entourent le philosophe.
4. Les touristes suivaient le guide.

Note de grammaire F: Le verbe *craindre*

The redundant **ne** poses some problems for American students. Remind them of a rhyme some of my students created to reinforce this point: "After positive fear and negative doubt, put in the **ne,** don't leave it out!"

Exercices de transformation

A. De quoi a-t-on peur?

Modèle: Il craint le froid. *(Tu)*
Tu crains le froid.

1. *Il* craint le froid. *(Je, Vous, Ils, On, Nous)*
2. *Il* a craint de s'enrhumer. *(Nous, Je, Vous, Tu, Ils)*
3. *Elle* craignait d'avoir de la fièvre. *(Ils, Nous, Tu, Je, Vous)*
4. *Je* craindrais d'être malade. *(Nous, Elle, Tu, Vous, Ils)*
5. Le professeur doute que *vous* craigniez les examens. *(on, je, nous, les étudiants, tu)*

B. Quand la nuit tombe.

Modèle: On plaint ceux qui n'ont pas d'imagination. *(Nous)*
Nous plaignons ceux qui n'ont pas d'imagination.

1. *J'*éteins la lampe. *(Nous, Tu, Mes amis, Il, Vous)*
2. *Quelques-uns* craignaient la nuit. *(Vous, Nous, Je, Tu, Elle)*
3. *L'imagination* a peint des images effrayantes. *(Nous, Vous, Elles, Tu, On)*
4. Atteindra-t-*on* la perfection en poésie? *(nous, Est-ce que je, ils, vous, tu)*

C. Modèle: Robert peint la maison. *(demain)*
Robert peindra la maison demain.

1. Robert peint la maison. *(aujourd'hui, hier, autrefois, s'il faisait beau, il faut que)*
2. Ils se plaignent du travail. *(souvent, toujours, la semaine prochaine, hier)*

3. J'ai craint de faire ça tout seul. *(demain, autrefois, ils ne sont pas contents que, maintenant, si je n'étais pas sûr de moi, hier)*

Travaux pratiques

Assign the following verbs to five students, who will work together to create a story following the Wave format: **craindre, peindre, éteindre, se plaindre, atteindre.**

Le monde francophone

This special section contains readings from and about the francophone world. Maps and photos augment the text and encourage discussions. The readings may be treated together as a separate unit or integrated into appropriate chapters of the main text. For example, the article **"La France géopolitique"** could be used in conjunction with the **Vocabulaire illustré** of **Chapitre 10** to provide further practice with names of countries, and the reading **"Le Sénégal"** could be used to expand on the **Micrologue** and **Lecture** about Léopold Sédar Senghor in **Chapitre 17.**

It is also possible to expand on each reading by assigning special research projects to individuals or teams. This works best when topics are limited to a fairly narrow area of investigation, such as popular gestures (what to do and what not to do), food, dating habits, and how people spend their leisure time. For example, in researching popular gestures in Algeria, students may discover that people greet both friends and strangers by handshakes and embraces, but that embraces are limited to members of the same sex. Hospitality is warm, genuine, and generous. In Algeria, as in other Moslem countries, it is impolite to point and to use the left hand alone. And when one is seated, it is considered offensive to show the soles of one's shoes.

Reinforcement Procedures

Teaching Scénarios

1. Première étape. This version of the dialogue, which is intended for comprehension only, isolates some of the basic elements of the **Scénario.** Have students look at the chapter-opening illustration while you read the dialogue several times. Students should not repeat the text but should understand it fairly well.

2. Deuxième étape. It is crucial for students to become thoroughly familiar with the **Deuxième étape** because the rest of the chapter—vocabulary, grammar notes, exercises, and activities—evolves from it. Based on your preference, students may continue to look at the chapter-opening illustration or work with books closed. Begin by presenting the entire dialogue, being as dramatic as possible. Exaggerated acting will make a strong impression on students and improve their recall. Next, present the text sentence by sentence, using backward build-up (that is, teaching each sentence in breath groups, starting from the end and progressing toward the beginning). Have the class repeat each breath group in chorus one or two times. Then have students repeat individually and end with several choral repetitions of the entire sentence. Here is an example based on **Chapitre 1:**

INSTRUCTOR: Deux étudiants / américains / vont en France.
Vont en France.
WHOLE CLASS: Vont en France.
INSTRUCTOR: Vont en France.
WHOLE CLASS: Vont en France.
INSTRUCTOR *(to individual):* Vont en France.
INDIVIDUAL: Vont en France.

Continue calling on individuals randomly. If a student does not respond correctly, seek a correct response from another student, congratulate him/her, and then have the first student repeat correctly. If two students in a row respond incorrectly, erase their errors by modeling the breath group once more and calling for choral repetition. Make sure that all students who make errors eventually produce the desired response. Then proceed to the next breath group:

INSTRUCTOR: Américains vont en France.
WHOLE CLASS: Américains vont en France.
INSTRUCTOR: Américains vont en France.
WHOLE CLASS: Américains vont en France.

Seek as many individual repetitions as time permits. Then practice the full sentence:

INSTRUCTOR: Deux étudiants américains vont en France.
WHOLE CLASS: Deux étudiants américains vont en France.
INSTRUCTOR: Deux étudiants américains vont en France.
WHOLE CLASS: Deux étudiants américains vont en France.

Once again elicit individual repetitions and then close the presentation of the first sentence with two choral repetitions.

Make sure that words with liaison are presented within the same breath group. For example, **vont en France** must be one unit because of the linkage between **vont** and **en**. Within a given sentence, remember to link each breath group to the preceding breath group, but do not link sentence to sentence. Proceed thusly through the **Deuxième étape,** from start to finish. Breath groups for the rest of the sentences would be:

Ils sont avec / un groupe. / Les amis / s'appellent / Robert et Henry./
Ils voyagent / ensemble. / [If you prefer liaison here, teach this as one group.]
Ils sont / dans un avion./
Ils décident / de parler / français./
L'hôtesse de l'air / apporte / les dîners./
Bonsoir. / Voici vos dîners. / Comment allez-vous?/
Je vais bien, / merci, / mais mon ami / va mal./
Est-ce que vous êtes fatigué / ou malade, / monsieur?/
Fatigué, / mademoiselle, / Oui, je suis / très fatigué./
Allez-vous dormir / ou regarder le film?/
Moi, je désire / regarder le film./
Moi, je désire / dormir. / N'oubliez pas / de me réveiller./
Bon appétit, / messieurs, / Je vais apporter les écouteurs./
Merci / et à tout à l'heure.

After such a systematic presentation, students should have fairly good control of the **Deuxième étape.** But do not expect perfection; rather, be satisfied with close renditions. Tell students that the next day they will act out the **Deuxième étape.** If you do not want your students to memorize the text, have them try to act out the events while recalling as much of the dialogue as possible or using their own words. Further practice of the **Deuxième étape** is presented on the *Audiotapes* and in the *Student Workbook/Laboratory Manual.*

3. Troisième étape. This optional version of the dialogue, which is intended for reading and comprehension only, brings the **Première** and **Deuxième étapes** into focus and introduces some new lexical items. If you decide to incorporate this feature into your presentation, explain new vocabulary and model the passage before having students read it aloud to practice fluency and intonation. To check understanding and expand vocabulary, have students paraphrase what they have read, perhaps incorporating terms from the **Synonymes et expressions approximatives** section presented in the *Student Workbook/Laboratory Manual.*

Optimizing Drills

1. Simples substitutions. The exercise sequences in this book often begin with simple substitution drills that are designed to build fluency, reinforce key structures and vocabulary, and demonstrate that language structures can be manipulated in a variety of ways. In a given drill, the substitutions always occur in the same, clearly stipulated part of the sentence—that is, at the beginning, in the middle, or at the end. In a typical simple substitution, the instructor begins by presenting a model consisting of the basic sentence, a sample cue, and the new combination:

INSTRUCTOR: *Les deux amis sont* dans un avion.
Nous sommes
Nous sommes dans un avion.

The instructor next reads the basic sentence again and has the class repeat it chorally:

INSTRUCTOR: *Les deux amis sont* dans un avion.
WHOLE CLASS: *Les deux amis sont* dans un avion.

The instructor then proceeds to give cues to individual students:

INSTRUCTOR: *Tu es*
STUDENT A: *Tu es* dans un avion.
INSTRUCTOR: *Henry est*
STUDENT C: *Henry est* dans un avion.
Etc.

Be sure to use appropriate gestures when giving cues. For example, to call for a choral response, you could use a brisk, upward sweep of the hands. By using gestures, you can avoid needless words that may interfere with the rhythm of the drill. For instance, when I present a substitution drill, I say the sentence: ***Les deux amis sont* dans un avion.** I then give the cue, ***nous sommes,*** point to myself, and respond: ***Nous sommes* dans un avion.** I usually accompany the pointing with a finger snap, which keeps students alert and establishes the pace of the drill. Finger snaps or tapping may also be used to establish the rhythm of a sentence and to indicate the breathing of each logical word group. Once students see what I want them to do during a drill, I proceed with the drilling process, trying to involve as many students as possible. If a student errs, I maintain rhythm by turning to another student for a correction.

2. Exercices de transformation. These drills provide more advanced grammatical practice by requiring students to reformulate elements of a sentence, usually by conjugating verbs or changing nouns to pronouns, singular to plural, affirmative to negative, declarative to interrogative, etc.

There are various kinds of transformation drills. Their cues take the same form as the cues for simple substitutions, and models clearly demonstrate the expected transformation. The key difference is that students do not merely slot the cue into the base sentence. Rather, they must use the cue to transform the base sentence. To implement a transformation drill, present the model yourself, emphasizing the desired transformation. Then proceed to give cues to individual students:

INSTRUCTOR: *Il* est dans l'avion.
Nous
Nous sommes dans l'avion.
Vous
STUDENT A: *Vous êtes* dans l'avion.
INSTRUCTOR: *Mon ami*
STUDENT B: *Mon ami est* dans l'avion.
Etc.

Audioscript

CHAPITRE PRELIMINAIRE

A. Prononciation: L'alphabet français avec l'alphabet phonétique international. There are 26 letters in the French alphabet. The columns below show the ways in which French is written and pronounced. The pronunciations are represented by Phonetic Alphabet. Repeat each letter after the speaker.

a	[a]	n	[en]
b	[be]	o	[o]
c	[se]	p	[pe]
d	[de]	q	[ky]
e	[ə]	r	[er]
f	[ɛf]	s	[es]
g	[ʒe]	t	[te]
h	[aʃ]	u	[y]
i	[i]	v	[ve]
j	[ʒi]	w	[dubləve]
k	[ka]	x	[iks]
l	[ɛl]	y	[igrɛk]
m	[ɛm]	z	[zɛd]

B. A l'aéroport. You are working at the Air France check-in counter. Listen carefully as people check in with you, giving their last names and spelling them out. Write each letter as you hear it.

1. Je m'appelle Mlle Lacoste.
2. Je m'appelle Mme Fourchet.
3. Je m'appelle M. Lorset.
4. Je m'appelle Mme Lavallée.
5. Je m'appelle M. Alençon.
6. Je m'appelle Mlle Prévert.
7. Je m'appelle M. Moïse.
8. Je m'appelle Mlle Jérôme.
9. Je m'appelle Mme Barrès.
10. Je m'appelle Mme Crozier.

C. L'itinéraire. Your friend Mark is leaving for a long tour of France. As he describes his itinerary for you, write the names of the places he'll visit.

1. Paris
2. Annecy
3. Chamonix
4. Avignon
5. Nîmes

D. Le professeur dit. You will hear a professor giving commands. Put the number of each command under the picture that best matches it.

1. Ouvrez le livre!
2. Asseyez-vous!
3. Tournez à gauche!
4. Fermez la porte!
5. Réveillez-vous!
6. Ouvrez la fenêtre!

E. En classe. Are the students in the pictures doing what their professor tells them to do? Listen as the professor gives each command. If it matches the picture, check **oui**; if not, check **non**.

1. Fermez le livre!
2. Levez-vous!
3. Réveillez-vous!
4. Ecoutez la musique!
5. Ouvrez la fenêtre!

This is the end of the taped activities for the preliminary chapter.

A. Scénario. Listen carefully to the conversation between Henry, Robert, and the flight attendant. You may not understand every word, but you should be able to follow the story line.

NARRATOR: Deux étudiants américains vont en France. Ils sont avec un groupe de camarades. Les amis s'appellent Robert et Henry. Ils voyagent ensemble. Ils sont dans un avion. L'avion vole vers la France. Ils décident de parler français. L'hôtesse de l'air apporte les dîners.
L'HOTESSE: Bonsoir. Voici vos dîners. Comment allez-vous?
HENRY: Je vais bien, merci, mais mon ami va mal.
L'HOTESSE: Est-ce que vous êtes fatigué ou malade, monsieur?
ROBERT: Fatigué, mademoiselle. Oui, je suis très fatigué.
L'HOTESSE: Allez-vous dormir ou regarder le film après le repas?
HENRY: Je vais regarder le film.
ROBERT: Moi, je désire dormir.
L'HOTESSE: D'accord. Bon appétit, messieurs. Je vais apporter les écouteurs.
HENRY: Merci et à tout à l'heure.

B. A vous maintenant! Listen again to the **scénario** and repeat during the pauses. Pay particular attention to pronunciation and intonation.

NARRATOR: Deux étudiants américains // vont en France. // Ils sont // avec un groupe de camarades. // Les amis s'appellent Robert et Henry. // Ils voyagent ensemble. // Ils sont dans un avion. // L'avion vole vers la France. // Ils décident de parler français. // L'hôtesse de l'air apporte // les dîners. //
L'HOTESSE: Bonsoir. // Voici vos dîners. // Comment allez-vous? //
HENRY: Je vais bien, // merci, // mais mon ami va mal. //
L'HOTESSE: Est-ce que vous êtes fatigué // ou malade, // monsieur? //
ROBERT: Fatigué, // mademoiselle. // Oui, je suis très fatigué. //
L'HOTESSE: Allez-vous dormir // ou regarder le film // après le repas? //
HENRY: Je vais regarder // le film. //
ROBERT: Moi, je désire dormir. //
L'HOTESSE: D'accord. // Bon appétit, // messieurs. // Je vais apporter // les écouteurs.//
HENRY: Merci // et à tout à l'heure. //

C. Prononciation: Le *h* muet versus le *h* aspiré. Listen to the discussion of the French letter **h** and repeat the key words and sentences during the pauses.

NARRATOR: In French, the letter **h** is never pronounced. In most cases, **h** at the beginning of a word is considered mute. The word is treated as if it begins with a vowel and there is elision or linking (**la liaison**). Listen carefully and repeat the following words.

l'homme --------> les hommes
l'hôtesse --------> les hôtesses

A word that begins with an aspirate **h** (**h aspiré**) is treated as though it begins with a consonant and there is no liaison. Listen carefully and repeat the following words.

le héros ---------> les héros
le Hongrois ----> les Hongrois
la haute couture les hors-d'œuvre

In dictionaries or printed vocabulary lists, a symbol is used to differentiate aspirate **h** from mute **h**. In this book we use an asterisk (*) to indicate an aspirate **h**.

Repeat the following sentences.

L'héroïne aime **le héros.**
La Hongroise et **l'homme** américain sont amis.
L'hôtesse apporte **les hors-d'œuvre.**

D. Le genre. Identify the gender of each noun you hear by circling **m** for **masculin** and **f** for **féminin.**

1. Voilà la fourchette.
2. Voilà une soucoupe.
3. Voilà le plateau.
4. Voilà la tasse.
5. Voilà un couteau.
6. Voilà une serviette.
7. Voilà la cuillère.
8. Voilà le verre.
9. Voilà le menu.
10. Voilà une assiette.

E. L'arbre généalogique. Study the family tree. Then comment on each statement you hear by checking **vrai** if it is true or **faux** if it is false. You will hear each statement twice.

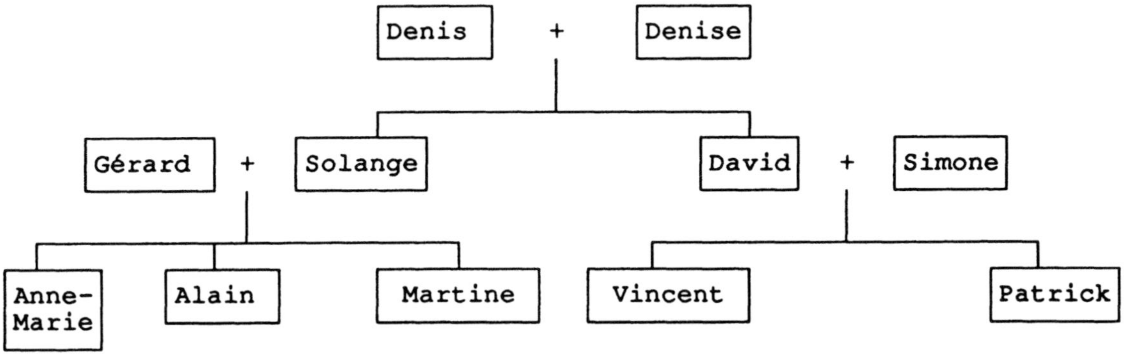

1. David est le frère de Patrick.
2. Simone est la tante d'Alain.
3. Denise est la grand-mère de Martine.
4. Gérard est l'oncle d'Anne-Marie.
5. Martine est la sœur de Vincent.
6. Solange est la fille de Denis et Denise.

F. Allons encore plus loin. Listen to the conversation between Robert, Henry, and Marguerite. Then, answer the following questions by circling the letter of the best response.

NARRATOR: Les deux amis arrivent à l'aéroport JFK à New York.
HENRY: Nous sommes en avance.
ROBERT: Oui, et il y a beaucoup de monde ici. Est-ce que tout le monde va en France?
HENRY: Non, pas possible. Les avions volent vers d'autres destinations. Regarde! Londres, Rome, Athènes.
ROBERT: Je suis fatigué.
HENRY: Je vais bien.
ROBERT: Voilà nos amis. Ah, voici Marguerite.
MARGUERITE: Bonjour!
ANNOUNCER: Flight 707 to Paris is now boarding.
MARGUERITE: A bientôt, à Paris.

1. Où les deux amis arrivent-ils?
   a. A La Guardia.
   b. A Charles de Gaulle.
   c. A JFK.

2. Est-ce qu'ils sont en avance?
   a. Oui.
   b. Non.

3. Y a-t-il beaucoup de monde?
   a. Oui.
   b. Non.

4. Est-ce que tout le monde va en France?
   a. Oui.
   b. Non.

5. Où est-ce que les avions volent?
   a. Vers d'autres destinations.
   b. Seulement à Paris.
   c. A New York.

6. Henry est-il fatigué?
   a. Oui.
   b. Non.

7. Où atterrit le vol 707?
   a. A new York.
   b. A Rome.
   c. A Paris.

G. Et pour finir. Listen to the conversation between Robert and Henry. Then, answer the following questions by circling the letter of the best response.

NARRATOR: A l'aéroport.
HENRY: Voici l'aéroport.
ROBERT: Je suis content d'être ici.
HENRY: Sommes-nous en retard?
ROBERT: Nous allons parler à cet homme.

1. Où les garçons sont-ils?
   a. Dans un avion.
   b. Dans une salle de classe.
   c. A l'aéroport.

2. Est-ce que Robert est content?
   a. Robert ne sait pas.
   b. Oui.
   c. On ne sait pas.

3. Henry est-il en avance?
   a. Henry n'est pas sûr.
   b. Oui.
   c. On ne sait pas.

4. Vont-ils parler à une femme?
   a. Oui.
   b. Non.
   c. On ne sait pas.

This is the end of the taped activities for Chapter 1.

A. Scénario. Listen carefully to the conversation between the students and the taxi driver. You may not understand every word, but you should be able to follow the story line.

NARRATOR: L'avion arrive à huit heures du matin. Les deux étudiants trouvent Marguerite, une camarade. Ils sont au service des bagages où ils cherchent les valises.
MARGUERITE: Je ne trouve pas ma raquette de tennis. Et vous, avez-vous toutes vos affaires?
ROBERT: Non, j'ai mes valises, mais je n'ai pas mon sac de couchage. *(Ils cherchent.)*
HENRY: Tiens, le voilà!
NARRATOR: Les trois jeunes gens trouvent l'autobus pour aller à l'aérogare. Là, ils trouvent un taxi.
ROBERT: Sommes-nous à la gare?
LE CHAUFFEUR: C'est ce que vous voulez, non? Vous y voilà!
ROBERT: Bien. Merci. Combien est-ce que je dois?
LE CHAUFFEUR: Cent cinquante francs et cinquante francs pour les bagages.
ROBERT: Voici deux cents francs.

B. A vous maintenant! Listen again to the **scénario** and repeat during the pauses. Pay particular attention to pronunciation and intonation.

NARRATOR: L'avion arrive // à huit heures du matin.// Les deux étudiants trouvent // Marguerite, une camarade.// Ils sont au service des bagages // où ils cherchent les valises.//
MARGUERITE: Je ne trouve pas // ma raquette de tennis.// Et vous,// avez-vous toutes vos affaires?//
ROBERT: Non, j'ai mes valises,// mais je n'ai pas mon sac de couchage.//
HENRY: Tiens, le voilà!//
NARRATOR: Les trois jeunes gens // trouvent l'autobus // pour aller à l'aérogare.// Là, ils trouvent un taxi.//
ROBERT: Sommes-nous à la gare?//
LE CHAUFFEUR: C'est ce que vous voulez, non?// Vous y voilà!//
ROBERT: Bien. Merci.// Combien est-ce que je dois?//
LE CHAUFFEUR: Cent cinquante francs // et cinquante francs // pour les bagages.//
ROBERT: Voici deux cents francs.//

C. Prononciation: Les voyelles. Listen to the discussion of French vowels and repeat the key words and sentences during the pauses.

1.[a]

table gare article la salade valise camarade bagages ami

L'article est sur la table.
Mon ami est assis et il mange de la salade.
A-t-il l'addition?

2.[e]

thé dîner pied répéter et aller nez rez-de-chaussée

J'ai mon pied dans le thé et mon nez dans le dîner.
Je vais aller au rez-de-chaussée.
L'école est fermée aujourd'hui. Allons jouer chez vous.

3.[ɛ]

père mère tête même frère après être mais lait laid billet ballet

Mon père et ma mère donnent un billet à l'homme.
Le jeune homme laid aime le lait mais non pas le ballet.
Etre ou ne pas être, là est la question!

4.[i]

si ici rire fini ami taxi mari midi

Si tu ris ici, mon ami, tu vas aller en taxi avec mon mari à midi.
Si six scies scient six cyprès / six cent six scies scient six cent six cyprès.

5.[o]

pot eau chaud beau couteau hôtesse

Je coupe l'eau dans le pot avec le couteau de l'hôtesse.
Le nouveau-né est beau.
Le troupeau est ici.

6.[ɔ]

robe notre homme comme Sorbonne dollar

Je donne un dollar à ma bonne.
Les robes à la Sorbonne sont courtes.
Veux-tu un pot, mon pote?

7.[u]

vous nous cou toujours couteau pourboire tout bonjour

Vous placez **toujours** le **pourboire** sur le **cou.**
Nous disons **toujours** bonj**our** avec un **couteau.**

D. Singulier ou pluriel? You will hear a series of subjects and verbs. Decide whether each pair is singular (**singulier**) or plural (**pluriel**) and check the appropriate column. If a subject and verb could be either singular or plural, check **pas clair**.

1. ils habitent
2. elle déjeune
3. elle écoute
4. il étudie
5. il ferme
6. elles aiment
7. ils arrivent
8. elle marche
9. elle apporte
10. elles oublient

E. Les prix. Listen as Alexandre and Caroline discuss some possible purchases. Then write the price of each item in the blank provided.

1. Alexandre: Combien coûte le magazine?
   Caroline: Le magazine coûte vingt francs.
   ____

2. Alexandre: Combien coûte un billet?
   Caroline: Un billet coûte quinze francs.
   ____

3. Alexandre: Combien coûte une carte postale?
   Caroline: Une carte postale coûte cinq francs.
   ____

4. Alexandre: Combien coûte le livre?
   Caroline: Le livre coûte seize francs.
   ____

5. Alexandre: Combien coûte le cahier?
   Caroline: Le cahier coûte douze francs.
   ____

6. Alexandre: Combien coûte un Coca?
   Caroline: Un Coca coûte dix francs.
   ____

F. Allons encore plus loin. You will hear a passage about a tourist's experience in a foreign country. Listen carefully as the passage is read twice. You will not understand every word, but you should be able to follow the story line. You will then hear a series of questions. Based on your understanding of the story, circle the letter of the best answer to each question. Read the textbook first.

Les touristes arrivent à l'aéroport de bonne heure. La police arrête les voyageurs et demande leurs passeports. L'agent de police vérifie les documents et le douanier demande si on a des choses à déclarer.

Le douanier: Ouvrez cette valise, s'il vous plaît.
Le touriste: Mais je n'ai rien à déclarer.
Le douanier: Ouvrez, ouvrez!
Le touriste: Mais je n'ai rien à déclarer.
Le douanier: Ouvrez, ouvrez! Montrez-moi l'intérieur de la valise.
Le touriste: Mais je n'ai rien à déclarer, monsieur.
Le douanier: Ouvrez cette valise, s'il vous plaît.
Le touriste ouvre la valise. Il n'y a rien dans la valise.

1. Est-ce que les touristes arrivent en retard?
   a. Non, ils arrivent en avance.
   b. Oui, ils arrivent en retard.
   c. Ils arrivent à l'aéroport.

2. Où est-ce qu'ils arrivent?
   a. Les touristes.
   b. En taxi.
   c. A l'aéroport.

3. Qu'est-ce que la police fait?
   a. La police mange des sandwiches.
   b. La police demande les passeports.
   c. Les touristes.

4. Que fait le douanier?
   a. Il vérifie les documents.
   b. Il ne déclare rien.
   c. Il demande si on a des choses à déclarer.

5. Qu'est-ce que le douanier dit?
   a. «Ouvrez la bouche!»
   b. «Ouvrez la porte!»
   c. «Ouvrez la valise!»

6. Pourquoi est-ce que le touriste n'ouvre pas la valise?
   a. Il n'a rien à déclarer.
   b. Il est malade.
   c. Il est dépaysé.

7. Qu'est-ce que le douanier dit de montrer?
   a. L'intérieur de sa poche.
   b. L'intérieur de son livre.
   c. L'intérieur de la valise.

8. Qu'est-ce qu'il y a à l'intérieur?
   a. Rien.
   b. Une déclaration.
   c. Un douanier.

This is the end of the taped activities for Chapter 2.

A. Scénario. Listen carefully to the students' conversations at the train station. You may not understand every word, but you should be able to follow the story line.

NARRATOR: Les trois amis sont bouleversés. Ils n'aiment pas ce chauffeur de taxi. Ils ramassent leurs affaires.
HENRY: Vite! Nous allons être en retard pour le train de neuf heures trois.
MARGUERITE: Quelle heure est-il?
HENRY: Il est neuf heures moins le quart.
MARGUERITE: Alors, nous sommes en avance.
NARRATOR: Au guichet...
ROBERT: Trois billets pour Bourges, s'il vous plaît.
L'EMPLOYE: Quelle classe? Aller et retour?
ROBERT: Est-ce que vous voulez dire... ?
L'EMPLOYE: (*exaspéré*) Allez, allez! Je suis occupé, moi! Il y a du monde. C'est un jour de congé.
ROBERT: (*désorienté*) Trois billets de seconde. Trois billets simples.
L'EMPLOYE: Quatre cent soixante francs.
ROBERT: (*intimidé*) Voici cinq cents francs.
L'EMPLOYE: Voici vos trois billets et votre monnaie, quarante francs. Dépêchez-vous! Le train est toujours à l'heure!

B. A vous maintenant! Listen again to the **scénario** and repeat during the pauses. Pay particular attention to pronunciation and intonation.

NARRATOR: Les trois amis // sont bouleversés.// Ils n'aiment pas // ce chauffeur de taxi.// Ils ramassent leurs affaires.//
HENRY: Vite!// Nous allons être en retard // pour le train // de neuf heures trois.//
MARGUERITE: Quelle heure est-il?//
HENRY: Il est neuf heures // moins le quart.//
MARGUERITE: Alors, // nous sommes en avance.//
NARRATOR: Au guichet... //
ROBERT: Trois billets pour Bourges,// s'il vous plaît.//
L'EMPLOYE: Quelle classe?// Aller et retour?//
ROBERT: Est-ce que vous voulez dire...?//
L'EMPLOYE: Allez, allez!// Je suis occupé, moi!// Il y a du monde.// C'est un jour de congé.//
ROBERT: Trois billets de seconde.// Trois billets simples.//
L'EMPLOYE: Quatre cent // soixante francs.//
ROBERT: Voici cinq cents francs.//
L'EMPLOYE: Voici vos trois billets // et votre monnaie,// quarante francs.// Dépêchez-vous!// Le train est toujours à l'heure!//

C. Prononciation: Le *e* muet. Listen to the discussion of the French mute **e** and repeat the key words and sentences during the pauses.

The mute **e**, written as an **e** without an accent, occurs quite often in French: **je, me, te, se, ce, de, ne.**

A mute **e** is pronounced in the initial syllable of a word beginning with a consonant. Listen carefully and repeat.

demain demander venir

It is not pronounced when it appears between two consonant sounds. Listen carefully and repeat.

souv~~e~~nir av~~e~~nue boul~~e~~vard

However, the **e** is pronounced when preceded by two or three consonants. Listen carefully and repeat.

justement premier notre votre vendredi

Pay special attention to the mute **e**'s in the following sentences and repeat during the pauses.

Vendredi, je vais aller au cinéma avec notre professeur.
C'est justement ce que je dis.
Le premier du mois est toujours intéressant.
Demain, nous allons regarder la télévision.

The unaccented **e** is not pronounced in certain contexts. Listen and repeat.

1. J~~e~~ veux faire la cuisin~~e~~.
2. Tu m~~e~~ dis toujours ça.
3. Nous décidons d~~e~~ parler.

D. En quelle saison sommes-nous? You will hear eight sentences. Write the number of each sentence below the picture it best describes. You may match more than one sentence to some of the pictures.

1. Aujourd'hui il fait chaud.
2. C'est le 14 juillet.
3. Tu aimes skier?
4. Il neige beaucoup.
5. On a les vacances de Noël.
6. C'est le 1er avril et il fait beau.
7. J'aime beaucoup les bikinis.
8. Nous sommes le 8 octobre et tous les étudiants sont en classe.

E. L'heure officielle. Listen as people use the 24-hour clock to tell what time it is. Decide if each time is A.M. or P.M. and check the appropriate column.

1. Il est dix-neuf heures.
2. Il est une heure et quart.
3. Il est dix heures et demie du matin.
4. Il est onze heures juste.
5. Il est quatorze heures.
6. Il est midi.
7. Il est vingt et une heures trente.
8. Il est deux heures moins le quart.
9. Il est treize heures.
10. Il est douze heures.

F. On va où? Six friends have different things to do, so each is going to a different place. Based on what each person plans to do, decide where he or she is going. Then draw a line connecting each name with the appropriate destination. Follow the model.

Modèle: Monique va regarder un film d'amour.
Monique va au cinéma.

1. Catherine va acheter des timbres.
2. Jacques va manger un sandwich.
3. Serge va prendre le train de dix heures.
4. Sylvie va acheter une nouvelle robe.
5. Pierre va acheter des cigares.

G. Maintenant ou plus tard (*later*)? You will hear descriptions of people's activities. Decide whether each action is taking place now or will take place later and check the appropriate column.

1. Nous allons voyager.
2. Elle écoute la musique.
3. Vous parlez anglais.
4. Tu vas manger de la pizza.
5. Je vais trouver un taxi.
6. On ferme la porte.
7. Ils arrivent à l'aéroport.
8. Elles vont à la boutique.

H. Allons encore plus loin. You will hear a passage that expands on this chapter's **scénario**. Listen carefully as the passage is read twice. You may not understand every word, but you should be able to follow the story line. You will hear a series of questions and possible answers. Based on your understanding of the story, circle the letter of the best answer to each question.

Les trois étudiants sont dans la salle d'attente où ils attendent le train. Ils demandent des renseignements au bureau de renseignements et ils déjeunent au buffet de la gare. Ils commandent des sandwiches. Bien sûr, ils réservent des places et enregistrent leurs bagages. La grande horloge sonne l'heure du départ. Ils montent dans le train. Les trois camarades évitent le wagon fumeur et cherchent leurs places réservées. Ils n'aiment pas la fumée. Le train commence à rouler et peu après ils sont contents du voyage.

1. Qu'est-ce que les trois étudiants attendent?
   a. Le train.
   b. La salle d'attente.
   c. Le garçon.

2. Où demandent-ils des renseignements?
   a. Au téléphone.
   b. Au bureau de renseignements.
   c. Au buffet.

3. Où déjeunent-ils?
   a. Dans le train.
   b. Sur la table.
   c. Au buffet.

4. Qu'est-ce qu'ils commandent?
   a. Des légumes.
   b. Des sandwiches.
   c. De la viande.

5. Qu'est-ce qu'ils réservent?
   a. Des valises.
   b. Des places.
   c. Des voitures.

6. Qu'est-ce qu'ils enregistrent?
   a. Les passeports.
   b. Les registres.
   c. Les bagages.

7. Qu'est-ce qui sonne l'heure?
   a. L'hôtesse de l'air.
   b. Le réveil-matin.
   c. La grande horloge.

8. Qu'est-ce qu'elle sonne?
   a. L'heure du départ.
   b. L'heure de l'arrivée.
   c. L'heure précise.

9. Pourquoi est-ce que les trois camarades ne vont pas dans le wagon fumeur?
   a. Parce qu'ils désirent fumer.
   b. Parce qu'ils aiment la fumée.
   c. Parce qu'ils n'aiment pas la fumée.

10. Est-ce qu'ils sont contents du voyage?
   a. On ne sait pas.
   b. Oui.
   c. Non.

This is the end of the taped activities for Chapter 3.

A. Scénario. Listen to the conversations between Henry, Marguerite, Robert, and a fellow passenger on the train. You may not understand every word, but you should be able to follow the story line.

NARRATOR: Robert, Henry et Marguerite discutent de l'employé de la gare et de son attitude. Le train commence à rouler. Ils regardent le paysage. Ils voient des choses intéressantes.
HENRI: Que va-t-on faire des billets?
ROBERT: Gardons les billets!
MARGUERITE: Ils sont compostés.
NARRATOR: Un vieux monsieur ouvre la portière du compartiment.
LE VIEUX MONSIEUR: La place est-elle libre?
ROBERT: Ah, oui, oui, (*il cherche la formule*) je vous en prie.
MARGUERITE: Pardon, monsieur, est-ce que Bourges est loin de Paris?
LE VIEUX MONSIEUR: Non, pas très loin, mademoiselle. Bourges est à deux cent vingt-cinq kilomètres de la capitale. Allez-vous étudier là-bas?
ROBERT: Oui, monsieur.
LE VIEUX MONSIEUR: Il y fait beau en été, mais il pleut beaucoup en hiver. On finit par s'y habituer.
ROBERT: Tu vois, Henry, ce monsieur est très gentil.

B. A vous maintenant! Listen again to the **scénario** and repeat during the pauses. Pay particular attention to pronunciation and intonation.

NARRATOR: Robert, Henry et Marguerite // discutent de l'employé de la gare // et de son attitude.// Le train commence à rouler.// Ils regardent le paysage.// Ils voient des choses // intéressantes.//
HENRI: Que va-t-on faire // des billets?//
ROBERT: Gardons les billets!//
MARGUERITE: Ils sont compostés.//
NARRATOR: Un vieux monsieur ouvre la portière // du compartiment.//
LE VIEUX MONSIEUR: La place // est-elle libre?//
ROBERT: Ah, oui, oui,// je vous en prie.//
MARGUERITE: Pardon, monsieur,// est-ce que Bourges // est loin de Paris?//
LE VIEUX MONSIEUR: Non, pas très loin,// mademoiselle.// Bourges est à deux cent// vingt-cinq kilomètres // de la capitale.// Allez-vous étudier // là-bas?//
ROBERT: Oui, monsieur.//
LE VIEUX MONSIEUR: Il y fait beau en été,// mais il pleut beaucoup // en hiver.// On finit // par s'y habituer.//
ROBERT: Tu vois, Henry,// ce monsieur est très gentil.//

C. Prononciation: Les sons [y], [ϕ] et [œ]. Listen to the discussion of the three French vowel sounds and repeat the key words and sentences during the pauses.

1. The sound [y] is pronounced with the mouth practically closed. The tongue is flat in the mouth and "swollen," while the lips are projected. Listen and repeat.

tu rue sur vu mur dur pur cure luxe bureau vendu ému du jus zut jupe

The sounds [i] and [y] are formed similarly except that the lips are rounded and they project to produce a [y], while the lips are drawn to the sides for [**i**]. Listen and repeat.

Tu roules contre un mur dur.
La rue me tue.
C'est sûr, tu es dur!
Je suis ému.
As-tu vendu ton bureau?
Zut! J'ai du jus sur ma jupe.

2. The sound [ϕ] is a closed sound. The mouth is in a position to pronounce a mute **e**, but the lips do not protrude as much and are rounded. Listen and repeat.

feu peu œufs heureux peux sérieux veux vieux deux queue jeu ceux

Du feu, s'il vous plaît.
Je veux deux œufs, mon vieux.
Sois sérieux, sois heureux: tu peux, tu sais.
Ceux qui participent au jeu ne font pas la queue.

3. The open sound vowel [œ] is pronounced with the mouth open. Note its occurrence in the following closed syllables:

professeur sœur peur œuf heure cœur beurre erreur mœurs leur

Je mange un œuf par jour.
Le professeur a deux sœurs.
Voltaire a dit: «Passe-moi le beurre».

D. Le temps et la météo. You will hear seven statements about the weather. If a statement is logical, check **vrai;** if it is not logical, check **faux.**

1. Quand il pleut, il y a des nuages.
2. Il pleut beaucoup dans le désert.
3. Il fait toujours froid en Floride.
4. Il neige souvent en été à Chicago.
5. On a souvent des éclairs et du tonnerre quand il fait beau.
6. Quand il fait un temps épouvantable, c'est très agréable.
7. On a souvent des éclairs et du tonnerre quand il fait de l'orage.

E. Qu'est-ce qu'on aime faire? You will hear descriptions of what five people like to do. Decide which of the following expressions best describes each person's actions and write its letter next to the number of the appropriate sentence.

a. faire la grasse matinée
b. faire du sport
c. faire la cuisine
d. faire des courses
e. faire la queue
f. faire du ski
g. faire des voyages
h. faire une promenade

1. Jacques adore aller à la soirée le vendredi soir, alors le samedi matin il aime...
2. Nathalie aime les montagnes et elle est très sportive, alors, elle aime...
3. Sylvie adore visiter des villes différentes et elle parle beaucoup de langues, alors, elle aime...
4. Caroline n'aime pas regarder les matchs de football à la télévision, mais elle adore jouer, alors, elle aime...
5. Etienne aime beaucoup préparer les dîners, alors, il aime...

F. Allons encore plus loin. You will hear a short conversation between three people on a train. You will hear seven questions, circle the correct answer for each question.

NARRATOR: Le train de 10h03 part pour Paris. Trois étudiants entrent dans le compartiment non-fumeurs.
HENRY: Pardon, madame, est-ce que ces places sont libres?
MME HERVET: Oui, monsieur, elles sont libres. Mais faites attention, s'il vous plaît! Vous êtes mouillés.
MARGUERITE: Désolée, madame. Il pleut à verse. Puis-je placer mes affaires dans le filet?
MME HERVET: Bien sûr, mademoiselle.

1. A quelle heure le train part-il?
   a. A dix heures trois du matin.
   b. A trois heures dix du matin.
   c. A deux heures trois du matin.

2. Qui entre dans le compartiment?
   a. Un étudiant.
   b. Trois étudiants.
   c. Trois étudiantes.

3. Fument-ils?
   a. Oui.
   b. Non.

4. Combien de personnes y a-t-il dans ce compartiment?
   a. Six.

b. Quatre.
c. Trois.

5. Où vont-ils probablement?
a. A Blois.
b. A Paris.
c. A Bourges.

6. Quel temps fait-il?
a. Il fait du soleil.
b. Il pleut à verse.
c. Il neige tout le temps.

7. Quel est le problème?
a. Ils sont humides.
b. Le champagne est sec.
c. Ils sont mouillés.

This is the end of the taped activities for Chapter 4.

A. Scénario. Listen carefully to the conversation at the train station in Bourges. You may not understand every word, but you should be able to follow the story line.

NARRATOR: Les trois amis arrivent à la gare de Bourges. Il y a beaucoup de monde à la gare. Il est onze heures vingt-deux et le train vient d'arriver. Les familles françaises sont déjà là. Plusieurs mères et pères sont inquiets parce qu'ils ne peuvent pas identifier leurs étudiants américains.
MME FOURCHET: Je crois reconnaître cet étudiant-là.
M. AUBRY: Voici mon jeune étudiant qui vient. Mais qu'il est différent!
M. CORNET: C'est vrai. Je ne peux pas l'identifier par sa photo.
MME BOYER: Ils sont grands et forts! On voit que tous les Américains sont très sportifs et prennent beaucoup de vitamines.
M. AUBRY: J'espère que le nouveau va être plus bavard que nos deux premiers étudiants.
MME FOURCHET: Et moi, j'espère qu'il ne va pas être si difficile à table.
NARRATOR: Le professeur américain consulte la liste des étudiants.
LE PROFESSEUR: (*Il les compte.*) ...dix-huit, dix-neuf, vingt. Enfin, ils sont tous là.

B. A vous maintenant! Listen again to the **scénario** and repeat during the pauses. Pay particular attention to pronunciation and intonation.

NARRATOR: Les trois amis arrivent // à la gare de Bourges.// Il y a beaucoup de monde // à la gare.// Il est onze heures vingt-deux // et le train vient d'arriver.// Les familles françaises sont déjà là.// Plusieurs mères et pères sont inquiets // parce qu'ils ne peuvent pas // identifier leurs étudiants américains.//
MME FOURCHET: Je crois reconnaître // cet étudiant-là.//
M. AUBRY: Voici mon jeune étudiant // qui vient.// Mais qu'il est différent!//
M. CORNET: C'est vrai.// Je ne peux pas // l'identifier par sa photo.//
MME BOYER: Ils sont grands et forts!// On voit que // tous les Américains sont// très sportifs // et prennent beaucoup de vitamines.//
M. AUBRY: J'espère que // le nouveau va être plus bavard // que nos deux premiers étudiants.//
MME FOURCHET: Et moi,// j'espère qu'il ne va pas être // si difficile à table.//
NARRATOR: Le professeur américain // consulte la liste des étudiants.//
LE PROFESSEUR: (*Il les compte.*) ...dix-huit, dix-neuf, vingt./ Enfin, ils sont tous là.//

C. Prononciation: Les sons [j], [ɥ] et [w]. Listen to the discussion of the French semivowels and repeat the key words and phrases during the pauses.

There are three semivowels (or semiconsonants) in French.

1. [j]. The semivowel **yod** often appears at the end of a word. Listen and repeat.

fille Bastille abeille travail feuille grenouille œil

Note, however, that **yod** does not appear in the following words. Listen and repeat.

m*ille* v*ille* tranqu*ille* G*ille*s L*ille*

2. [ɥ]. The semivowel [ɥ] occurs when a vowel other than mute **e** follows the letter **u**. Both [ɥ] and the vowel sound are quickly pronounced. Listen and repeat.

nuit fruit suis nuage juin

3. [**w**]. The semivowel [**w**] occurs in the letter combination **oi** and when **ou** is followed by a vowel other than mute **e**. Listen and repeat.

oui moi toi jouons coin fois

Une **fille** traverse le seu**il** de la Basti**lle** avec sa fami**lle**.
Une abe**ille** n'est jamais tranqu*ille*; elle trava**ille** tout le temps.
G*ille*s et les grenou**illes** sont tranqu*ille*s dans la v*ille* de L*ille*.
Des feu**illes** tombent sans **bruit** au mil**ieu** de la **nuit**.
Jouons au **coin** de la maison, **loin** des **nuages** du **mois** de **juin**.

D. Comment sont-ils? You'll hear a statement about each picture. If the statement is true, write **v (vrai)**; if it is false, write **f (faux)** in the blank provided.

1. Ils jouent bien au basket parce qu'ils sont petits et gros.
2. Ils sont très forts et musclés.
3. Ils sont très laids comme tous les acteurs célèbres.
4. Ils sont laids.
5. Ils sont très faibles et restent toujours au lit.
6. Ils sont gros, alors ils font beaucoup d'exercices.
7. Ils sont gros.

E. Où est le chien? Où va-t-il? You will hear eleven sentences describing the location of the dog. Write the number of each sentence next to the picture it best describes.

1. Il va tout droit.
2. Il est sur la table.
3. Il est à gauche de la porte.
4. Il est en haut de l'escalier.
5. Il est sous la table.
6. Il est au bout du couloir.
7. Il est à droite de la porte.
8. Il est près de la porte.
9. Il est loin de la porte.
10. Il va à droite.
11. Il va à gauche.

F. Singulier ou pluriel? You will hear three people talking about what they are doing with certain things. Listen carefully and decide whether each sentence is about one thing or more than one and place a check in the appropriate column.

Nathalie

1. J'achète des timbres.
2. Je mets un timbre sur l'enveloppe.
3. Je poste la lettre à notre frère.

Isabelle

4. Je choisis une robe à la boutique.
5. J'achète des robes et des jupes.
6. Je porte une robe bleue à la partie.

Sophie

7. Je regarde des sandwiches.
8. Je choisis des sandwiches délicieux.
9. Je mange un sandwich au jambon.
10. Je mets le sandwich au fromage dans mon sac.

G. Soyez logique! You will hear questions about why five people want to do certain things. Decide which of the following expressions best explains the reason for each person's desire and indicate its letter to answer the appropriate question. Follow the model.

a. a faim
b. a peur
c. a sommeil
d. a mal à la tête
e. a soif

Modèle: Pourquoi est-ce que Jean veut un sandwich?
NARRATOR: The correct answer is **(a)** : Jean veut un sandwich *parce qu'il a faim.*

1. Pourquoi est-ce que Sophie veut un Coca?
2. Pourquoi est-ce que Philippe veut dormir?
3. Pourquoi est-ce que Victor ne veut pas regarder le film d'horreur?
4. Pourquoi est-ce que Julie veut une omelette?
5. Pourquoi est-ce que Martine veut de l'aspirine?

H. Récemment ou bientôt? Listen as some parents brag about their babies. If the parent is talking about the recent past, check **récemment;** if he or she is talking about the future, check **bientôt.**

1. Il vient de faire ses premiers pas.
2. Il vient de parler français.
3. Elle va parler japonais.
4. Elle vient de dire «maman».
5. Il va dire «épouvantable».
6. Elle vient de manger des bananes.
7. Elle va manger une pomme.
8. Elle vient de jouer à cache-cache.
9. Il va jouer au football américain.
10. Il vient de danser.

I. En faisant les courses. Où se terminent-elles? You will hear the routes four people take as they run their errands. All start at the supermarket on rue Emile Desvaux. Use the map to follow each person's progress. Then write his or her destination next to the appropriate name.

1. Sylvie est très pressée parce qu'elle a beaucoup à faire. D'abord, elle va à la station-service à côté, puis elle tourne à droite et traverse le pont. Tout de suite après avoir traversé la rivière, elle tourne à gauche. Elle va au deuxième magasin à droite où elle achète des vitamines et du shampooing. Où est-elle?

2. Nathalie sort du supermarché et elle prend l'avenue du Général de Gaulle. Elle tourne à gauche dans la rue de la République où elle achète des timbres. Elle retourne ensuite dans l'avenue du Général de Gaulle et continue vers l'église, mais elle ne tourne pas à gauche dans la rue de l'Abbaye, elle va plutôt à droite. Elle arrête la voiture et va chercher ses filles qui jouent au foot. Où est-elle?

3. David va d'abord à la bibliothèque dans la rue Emile Desvaux. Il tourne ensuite à droite deux fois et se retrouve à la banque. Il continue tout droit et va dans le bâtiment à gauche où il attend sa mère qui va arriver de Marseille. Où est-il?

4. Pierre va au café où il a rendez-vous avec un ami. Ils repartent ensemble. Ils prennent la rue de l'Abbaye, tournent à droite et tournent à gauche dans la troisième rue. Ils entrent dans le bâtiment à gauche au bout de la rue où ils vont passer l'après-midi. Où sont-ils?

J. Allons encore plus loin. You will hear a passage that expands on this chapter's vocabulary and grammar. Listen carefully as the passage is read twice. You may not understand every word, but you should be able to follow the story line. You will then hear a series of questions and possible answers. Based on your understanding of the story, circle the letter of the best answer to each question.

Deux messieurs forts, beaux et costauds, sont près de la porte, en bas de l'escalier. Ils quittent la maison, cherchent leur voiture et traversent le pont. Ils arrivent chez leurs amis. Ils sont étonnés de voir leurs neveux avec des chevaux devant le château. Leurs neveux viennent tout de suite. Ils ont soif et ils ont envie de boire de l'eau.

1. Comment peut-on décrire les messieurs?
   a. Forts.
   b. Maigres.
   c. Laids.

2. Où sont-ils au début?
   a. Loin de la porte.
   b. En bas de la porte.
   c. En bas de l'escalier.

3. Qu'est-ce qu'ils cherchent?
   a. La maison.
   b. Leur bureau.
   c. Leur voiture.

4. Qu'est-ce qu'ils traversent?
   a. Le pont.
   b. Leur voiture.
   c. Leurs amis.

5. Pourquoi sont-ils étonnés?
   a. Ils voient leurs neveux avec des cheveux devant le château.
   b. Ils voient leurs neveux avec des chevaux devant le château.
   c. Ils voient leurs neveux avec des chevaux derrière le château.

6. Que font leurs neveux?
   a. Ils viennent plus tard.
   b. Ils viennent avant.
   c. Ils viennent tout de suite.

7. Pourquoi ont-ils envie de boire?
   a. Parce qu'ils ont faim.
   b. Parce qu'ils ont chaud.
   c. Parce qu'ils ont soif.

This is the end of the taped activities for Chapter 5.

A. Scénario. Listen carefully to the conversations as Robert meets the Fourchet family and sees his new room. You may not understand every word, but you should be able to follow the story line.

NARRATOR: Robert monte dans la petite «deux chevaux» de Mme Fourchet. Elle le conduit chez elle. Tout à coup, il commence à pleuvoir.
MME FOURCHET: Je suis désolée, il pleut souvent.
ROBERT: Ça ne fait rien.
MME FOURCHET: Il va faire beau demain.
NARRATOR: Ils arrivent chez les Fourchet.
MME FOURCHET: Olivier, voici notre jeune étudiant américain.
M. FOURCHET: (*Il serre la main de Robert.*) Je le reconnais, nous avons sa photo. Bonjour!
ROBERT: Bonjour, monsieur... (*Il réussit à trouver la formule.*) Je suis heureux de faire votre connaissance.
M. FOURCHET: Et voici notre fille, Nicole.
ROBERT: Bonjour, Nicole.
MME FOURCHET: Venez, Robert, je vais vous montrer votre chambre.
NARRATOR: Ils montent au premier étage et entrent dans la chambre de Robert.
MME FOURCHET: La voici. Elle est grande, n'est-ce pas? Dans ce placard vous avez des serviettes propres.
ROBERT: (*gêné*) Madame, euh! Puis-je...
MME FOURCHET: Oui, ah, oui. Les W.-C. sont au bout du couloir.
ROBERT: *(soulagé)* Oui, les W.-C., merci.
MME FOURCHET: Il y a du savon sur le lavabo, Robert, et une serviette sur le porte-serviettes.

B. A vous maintenant! Listen again to the **scénario** and repeat during the pauses. Pay particular attention to pronunciation and intonation.

NARRATOR: Robert monte dans la petite «deux chevaux» // de Mme Fourchet.// Elle le conduit chez elle.// Tout à coup,// il commence à pleuvoir.//
MME FOURCHET: Je suis désolée,// il pleut souvent.//
ROBERT: Ça ne fait rien.//
MME FOURCHET: Il va faire beau demain.//
NARRATOR: Ils arrivent chez les Fourchet.//
MME FOURCHET: Olivier, voici notre jeune étudiant // américain.//
M. FOURCHET: Je le reconnais, nous avons sa photo.// Bonjour!//
ROBERT: Bonjour, monsieur.// Je suis heureux de faire // votre connaissance.//
M. FOURCHET: Et voici notre fille, Nicole.//
ROBERT: Bonjour, Nicole.//
MME FOURCHET: Venez, Robert,// je vais vous montrer votre chambre.//

NARRATOR: Ils montent au premier étage // et entrent dans la chambre de Robert.//

MME FOURCHET: La voici.// Elle est grande,// n'est-ce pas?// Dans ce placard// vous avez des serviettes propres.//

ROBERT: Madame, euh!// Puis-je... //

MME FOURCHET: Oui, ah, oui.// Les W.-C. sont au bout // du couloir.//

ROBERT: Oui, les W.-C., merci.//

MME FOURCHET: Il y a du savon // sur le lavabo,// Robert,// et une serviette// sur le porte-serviettes.//

C. Prononciation: Les voyelles nasales. Listen carefully to the discussion of French nasal vowels and repeat the key words during the pauses.

NARRATOR: There are four nasal vowels in French: [œ̃], [ɔ̃], [ɛ̃], [ɑ̃]. The word *nasal* is misleading when it leads people to believe that French is best spoken when one has a cold. Actually, only a minor amount of air passes through the nasal passages when these vowel sounds are pronounced. Listen and repeat.

1. [œ̃]

   un l**un**di br**un** parf**um** chac**un**

   Le l**un**di chac**un** porte **un** parf**um** br**un**.

2. [ɔ̃]

   on **on**ze b**on** n**om** **on**cle b**on**b**on**

   On a vu m**on** grand **on**cle le **on**ze avril quand il mangeait des b**on**b**ons**.

3. [ɛ̃]

   v**in** **im**possible p**ain** f**aim** rais**in**

   Il est **im**possible d'avoir f**aim** quand on mange du p**ain** et quand on boit du v**in**.

4. [ɑ̃]

   bl**an**c cam**em**bert l**en**t l**am**pe Je**an**

   Je**an** Lebl**an**c qui est très l**en**t m**an**ge du cam**em**bert sous la l**am**pe.

5. **nasal** (mixed)

   Le l**un**di m**on** gr**an**d **on**cle Je**an** Lebl**an**c fait l'**im**possible et m**an**ge du cam**em**bert br**un** au rais**in**.

Note that a vowel is not nasalized when **n** or **m** is followed by a vowel and pronounced in the following syllable. Listen and repeat.

mon bon **ami** inoubliable

The same is true if the **n** or **m** is doubled:

immédiat **in**nocent

D. Les objets. You will hear six sentences that contain direct object pronouns. Decide whether each direct object pronoun refers to a masculine, feminine, or plural noun and check the appropriate column.

1. Je la vois.
2. Ils les regardent souvent.
3. Elle le désire depuis longtemps.
4. Stéphane va la chercher.
5. Nous les trouvons difficiles.
6. Est-ce que vous le détestez toujours?

E. Descriptions. You will hear eight sentences that describe people and things. Decide whether each person or thing is (1) masculine or feminine, and (2) singular or plural, and check the appropriate columns. ***Note*** that you should check two columns for each sentence.

1. C'est une bonne fille.
2. Nous préférons les petites motos.
3. Tu n'aimes pas les vilaines abeilles.
4. Mes copains ne connaissent pas la nouvelle étudiante.
5. J'ai un grand frère.
6. Serge va acheter une grosse voiture.
7. Allez-vous acheter un nouveau disque?
8. Ils détestent la vieille auto.

F. La maison. You will hear ten statements about the contents of the following house. If a statement is true, check **vrai;** if it is false, check **faux.**

1. La table est dans la chambre.
2. Le lavabo est dans la salle de bains.
3. Il y a une corbeille à papier aux W.-C.
4. Le micro-ondes est dans la cuisine.
5. Il y a un bureau dans le bureau.
6. Il y a une douche dans la salle de séjour.
7. Les draps et la couverture sont sur la table.
8. Il y a un tableau dans la salle de séjour.
9. Le buffet est dans la salle à manger.
10. La chambre est au deuxième étage.

G. Ça se fait où? You will hear eight sentences describing what people are doing. Draw a line from each person's name to the place he or she is most likely to be while performing the activity. ***Note*** that more than one activity may take place in some rooms. Follow the model.

Modèle: Jean écoute la musique.
Il est dans la salle de séjour.

1. Victor prépare le dîner.
2. Sylvie et Pierre déjeunent.
3. Madeleine est fatiguée. Elle fait la grasse matinée.
4. Serge étudie.
5. Suzette a rendez-vous dans une heure; elle prend donc une douche.
6. Marc fait le lit.
7. Les enfants regardent la télé.
8. Charles cherche le dictionnaire.

H. Allons encore plus loin. You will hear a passage that expands on this chapter's vocabulary and grammar. Listen carefully as the passage is read twice. You may not understand every word, but you should be able to follow the story line. You will then hear a series of questions and possible answers. Based on your understanding of the story, circle the letter of the best answer to each question.

Dans la chambre, il y a un lit. Sur le lit, il y a des draps, une couverture et un oreiller. Dans la salle à manger, il y a un buffet. On met les repas sur une table et on s'assied sur une chaise. Dans le salon, on regarde la télévision assis dans un fauteuil, et on écoute de la musique sur une chaîne stéréo. Dans la salle de bains, on prend une douche. Dans le bureau, on répond au téléphone et on prépare des rapports sur un ordinateur. On jette les papiers dans une corbeille à papier.

1. Qu'est-ce qu'il y a dans la chambre?
   a. Un lavabo.
   b. Un micro-ondes.
   c. Un lit.

2. Qu'est-ce qu'on met sur le lit?
   a. Des draps, une couverture et un oreiller.
   b. Des draps, une couleur et une oreille.
   c. Des draps, une coutume et un oreiller.

3. Comment appelle-t-on l'objet où on met son oreille?
   a. Un oreiller.
   b. Un orteil.
   c. Une cuillère.

4. Que peut-on trouver dans la salle à manger?
   a. Un tapis, une table et une chaise.

b. Un buffet, une table et une chaise.
c. Une bouteille, une table et une chaise.

5. Que peut-on faire dans le salon?
   a. Regarder la télévision et écouter de la musique.
   b. Regarder la télévision et regarder la chaîne stéréo.
   c. Regarder la télévision et sentir des fleurs.

6. Que peut-on faire dans la salle de bains?
   a. Prendre une douche.
   b. Vendre une douche.
   c. Rendre une douche.

7. Quel travail fait-on dans le bureau?
   a. On répond au téléphone et on dort.
   b. On répond au téléphone et on prépare des rapports.
   c. On répond au téléphone et on prépare des crêpes.

8. Où jette-t-on des papiers?
   a. Par la fenêtre.
   b. Dans le lavabo.
   c. Dans une corbeille à papier.

This is the end of the taped activities for Chapter 6.

A. Scénario. Listen carefully to the lunch-time conversation at the Fourchet house. You may not understand every word, but you should be able to follow the story line.

NARRATOR: M. Fourchet rentre chez lui pour déjeuner. Il va retourner travailler dans deux heures et il a faim. A table, Mme Fourchet sert les hors-d'œuvre.
MME FOURCHET: Aimez-vous les tomates et les concombres?
ROBERT: Oui, je les aime bien.
MME FOURCHET: Prenez du pain, aussi.
M. FOURCHET: Un instant. Nicole, donne-moi cette bouteille. On va porter un toast au succès de ce jeune homme. A votre santé!
(Robert ne répond pas.)
MME FOURCHET: Robert, vous répondez: «A la vôtre!».
ROBERT: A la vôtre!
NICOLE: Aimes-tu le vin blanc?
ROBERT: Oh, oui! *(Il boit le vin d'un trait.)*
NICOLE: Tu l'as bu comme de l'eau.
ROBERT: C'est vrai. J'ai très soif.
NARRATOR: Mme Fourchet a apporté le rôti.
ROBERT: Ah, encore...
MME FOURCHET: Voici un gigot et des haricots. Après il y a du fromage: aujourd'hui, c'est un camembert. Ensuite, nous allons te tutoyer.

B. A vous maintenant! Listen again to the **scénario** and repeat during the pauses. Pay particular attention to pronunciation and intonation.

NARRATOR: M. Fourchet rentre chez lui // pour déjeuner.// Il va retourner travailler // dans deux heures // et il a faim.// A table, Mme Fourchet sert les hors-d'œuvre.//
MME FOURCHET: Aimez-vous // les tomates et les concombres?//
ROBERT: Oui, je les aime bien.//
MME FOURCHET: Prenez du pain, aussi.//
M. FOURCHET: Un instant.// Nicole, donne-moi // cette bouteille.// On va porter un toast // au succès // de ce jeune homme.// A votre santé!//
MME FOURCHET: Robert, vous répondez:// «A la vôtre!».//
ROBERT: A la vôtre!//
NICOLE: Aimes-tu // le vin blanc?//
ROBERT: Oh, oui!//
NICOLE: Tu l'as bu // comme de l'eau.//
ROBERT: C'est vrai.// J'ai très soif.//
NARRATOR: Mme Fourchet a apporté le rôti.//
ROBERT: Ah, encore... //
MME FOURCHET: Voici un gigot // et des haricots.// Après il y a du fromage:// aujourd'hui, // c'est un camembert.// Ensuite, nous allons te tutoyer.//

C. Prononciation: L'élision. Listen carefully to the following and repeat during the pauses.

Elision occurs when the final **-e** or **-a** of certain short words, such as **le, la, de, je,** and **que**, is dropped before a word beginning with a vowel or mute **h.** Listen and repeat.

L'enfant fait du ski.
L'école est à droite.
J'ai le sac.
Je **n'ai** pas **d'argent.**
Je **n'ai** pas le livre.
Est-ce **qu'elle** vient?

The **-i** of **si** is dropped when the following word begins with **i**, as in **s'il** or **s'ils.** Listen and repeat.

S'il vient, nous partons ensemble.
S'ils ont faim, ils vont au restaurant.

D. En Italie. Michel, a French college student, is participating in a summer program in Italy. Halfway through his stay he calls his brother to tell him about his visit. Decide whether each of his statements describes something he has done already (**déjà fait**), or something he is planning to do (**projeté**), and check the appropriate column.

1. Nous avons beaucoup voyagé.
2. Je vais voir tout ce qui est important, je crois.
3. J'ai visité Rome pendant la première semaine.
4. D'autres étudiants et moi, nous avons pris le train.
5. La prochaine fois, je vais aller tout seul.
6. Nous avons vu le Vatican. C'est magnifique!
7. J'ai déjà mangé beaucoup de pizza et de spaghettis.
8. Je vais grossir, je crois!

E. De la vitamine C... You will hear ten statements about fruits and vegetables. Write the number of each statement under the item to which it refers.

1. Moi, j'adore les asperges. Elles ont un goût inhabituel et délicieux.
2. Les enfants n'aiment pas les épinards en général.
3. Les poivrons peuvent être verts, rouges, jaunes et même oranges.
4. Les artichauts sont assez exotiques.
5. Les frites sont faites à base de pommes de terre.
6. L'ail est essentiel dans la cuisine italienne.
7. Les aubergines sont des légumes violets.
8. Les choux sont des légumes, c'est vrai, mais on peut aussi appeler une personne que l'on aime «mon chou».

9. La soupe aux poireaux est très populaire en hiver.
10. Les concombres poussent bien avec beaucoup de soleil.

F. Au marché. You are sitting on the terrace of a café facing the market. Match each price you hear a vendor or waiter call out with the item to which it refers.

1. Les poulets: dix euros chacun.
2. L'apéritif coûte quarte euros, monsieur.
3. Les pamplemousses: deux euros cinquante le kilo!
4. Les cerises sont très belles et délicieuses, messieurs et mesdames! Seulement six euros le kilo.
5. C'est deux euros la bière, s'il vous plaît!
6. Le veau est à quinze euros le kilo.
7. Les poires sont superbes! Trois euros quarante le kilo; très bon marché!.
8. L'ananas, cinq euros la pièce.
9. Les bananas sont les meilleures de la saison! Deux euros trente le kilo! Venez! Venez!
10. Le thé coûte trois euros.

G. L'alimentation. You'll hear descriptions of the things that six people want to buy. Say where they have to go to get them. Follow the model.

Modèle: Serge voudrait acheter du fromage.
Il va à la crémerie.

1. Angélique voudrait acheter des crevettes et du thon.
2. Alice voudrait acheter du pâté.
3. Marc voudrait acheter du sel et du poivre.
4. Annette voudrait acheter une baguette.
5. Marguerite voudrait acheter les tartes au citron et un gâteau.
6. Daniel voudrait acheter un rôti.

H. Allons encore plus loin. You will hear a passage that expands on this chapter's vocabulary and grammar. Listen carefully as the passage is read twice. You may not understand every word, but you should be able to follow the story line. You will then hear a series of questions and possible answers. Based on your understanding of the story, circle the letter of the best answer to each question.

Les Fourchet vont au restaurant avec Robert. Ils ont faim. Ils veulent commander un repas délicieux. Il y a du monde et les gens sont serrés comme des sardines. Un garçon, haut comme trois pommes, recommande la pizza. M. Fourchet préfère les nouilles et il répète plusieurs fois ce qu'il désire. Le garçon n'y comprend rien: c'est une véritable nouille. Robert le dit et il reçoit un marron. Mme Fourchet tombe dans les pommes et M. Fourchet ne laisse pas de pourboire.

1. Avec qui les Fourchet vont-ils au restaurant?
   a. Avec Henriette.
   b. Avec Roberte.
   c. Avec Robert.

2. Pourquoi vont-ils au restaurant?
   a. Parce qu'ils ont le temps.
   b. Parce qu'ils sont fins.
   c. Parce qu'ils ont faim.

3. Qu'est-ce qu'ils veulent?
   a. Un repas succulent.
   b. Un repas délicieux.
   c. Un repas débile.

4. Qu'y a-t-il dans le restaurant?
   a. Des sardines.
   b. Des garçons.
   c. Du monde.

5. Est-ce que le garçon est grand?
   a. Oui.
   b. Non.

6. Que recommande le garçon?
   a. Des sardines.
   b. Des nouilles.
   c. La pizza.

7. Que préfère M. Fourchet?
   a. Les nouilles.
   b. Les sardines.
   c. Les nougats.

8. Que fait M. Fourchet?
   a. Il mange des nouilles.
   b. Il répète plusieurs fois.
   c. Il répète une fois.

9. Pourquoi le garçon ne comprend-il pas?
   a. Il ne fait pas attention.
   b. Il mange des nouilles.
   c. C'est une véritable nouille.

10. Que fait Robert?
    a. Il ne fait rien.
    b. Il dit que le garçon est une nouille.
    c. Il mange des nouilles.

11. Qu'est-ce qu'il reçoit?
    a. Il reçoit un marron.
    b. Il reçoit une marque.
    c. Il reçoit une malle.

12. Que fait Mme Fourchet?
    a. Elle mange des pommes.
    b. Elle tombe dans les pommes.
    c. Elle donne des pommes.

13. Que fait M. Fourchet?
    a. Il ne laisse pas de pourboire.
    b. Il laisse un pourboire.
    c. Il commande des boissons.

This is the end of the taped activities for Chapter 7.

A. Scénario. Listen carefully to the conversations as Robert settles in with the Fourchet Family. You may not understand every word, but you should be able to follow the story line.

NARRATOR: Robert est dans sa chambre. Mme Fourchet l'aide à s'installer et à vider ses valises.
MME FOURCHET: J'ai placé tes affaires dans cette armoire. Combien de valises as-tu? Est-ce tout?
ROBERT: Oui. J'ai cette grande valise grise, cette petite valise marron et ce sac de couchage que j'ai perdu et retrouvé finalement.
MME FOURCHET: J'ai placé tes chemises dans ce tiroir... tes slips et tes tee-shirts ici... tes mouchoirs et tes chaussettes là... ton veston et ton imperméable dans la penderie.
NARRATOR: Elle regarde ses valises.
MME FOURCHET: Vraiment, tu as de jolies valises. Elles sont plus solides que mes valises.
ROBERT: Je les aime bien. Ma mère me les a données.
MME FOURCHET: Comme tu as vu, tu as un lavabo. Tu peux faire ta toilette ici et prendre tes douches dans cette salle de bains.
NARRATOR: Mme Fourchet et Robert descendent au rez-de-chaussée.
M. FOURCHET: Je pars. Robert, tu peux emprunter une de nos mobylettes durant ton séjour. Nicole va te montrer comment elle marche. Nicole, montre-lui surtout comment freiner.
ROBERT: Pourquoi insiste-t-il là-dessus?
NICOLE: Evidemment si on ne sait pas freiner on peut avoir des problèmes.
NARRATOR: Les jeunes gens sortent.
MME FOURCHET: *(criant)* Nicole, passe par la boulangerie et achète une baguette, s'il te plaît!

B. A vous maintenant! Listen again to the **scénario** and repeat during the pauses. Pay particular attention to pronunciation and intonation.

NARRATOR: Robert est dans sa chambre.// Mme Fourchet l'aide à s'installer // et à vider ses valises.//
MME FOURCHET: J'ai placé tes affaires // dans cette armoire.// Combien de valises as-tu?// Est-ce tout?//
ROBERT: Oui.// J'ai cette grande valise grise,// cette petite valise marron // et ce sac de couchage // que j'ai perdu // et retrouvé finalement.//
MME FOURCHET: J'ai placé tes chemises // dans ce tiroir... // tes slips et tes tee-shirts ici... // tes mouchoirs et tes chaussettes là... // ton veston et ton imperméable // dans la penderie.//
NARRATOR: Elle regarde ses valises.//

MME FOURCHET: Vraiment,// tu as de jolies valises.// Elles sont plus solides // que mes valises.//

ROBERT: Je les aime bien.// Ma mère me les a données.//

MME FOURCHET: Comme tu as vu,// tu as un lavabo.// Tu peux faire ta toilette ici // et prendre tes douches // dans cette salle de bains.//

NARRATOR: Mme Fourchet et Robert descendent // au rez-de-chaussée.//

M. FOURCHET: Je pars.// Robert,// tu peux emprunter une de nos mobylettes // durant ton séjour.// Nicole va te montrer // comment elle marche.// Nicole,// montre-lui surtout // comment freiner.//

ROBERT: Pourquoi insiste-t-il là-dessus?//

NICOLE: Evidemment // si on ne sait pas freiner // on peut avoir des problèmes.//

NARRATOR: Les jeunes gens sortent.//

MME FOURCHET: *(criant)* Nicole,// passe par la boulangerie // et achète une baguette,// s'il te plaît!//

C. Prononciation: Syllabation. Listen to the discussion of French syllabication and repeat the key words during the pauses.

1. French syllables, wherever possible, begin with a consonant. Listen and repeat.

   fa-cile **che**-val é-**co**le **dî**-ner **re**-pas

2. Some consecutive consonants may be separated to begin new syllables. Listen and repeat.

   lais-**ser** ad-**jec**-tif gouver-**ne**-ment con-**clu**-sion

3. The combinations **ch, ph, th, gn,** and any consonant plus **l** or **r** may not be separated. Listen and repeat.

   four-**chet**-te **phi**-lo-so-**phe** ca-**tho**-li-que ma-**gni**-fi-que fai-**ble**
   ap-**pli**-ca-tion **dra**-peau com-**pren**-**dre** **tra**-vaux

D. Les vêtements, s'il vous plaît! You will hear descriptions of six people's outfits. Write each person's name under his or her picture according to the description that best fits.

1. Madeline porte une jupe, un tee-shirt et des lunettes de soleil.
2. Chantal porte un short, des tennis et une blouse imprimée fleurs.
3. Serge porte un pantalon, une chemise, des socquettes et des chaussures.
4. Michel porte un maillot de bain rayé.
5. Monique porte un tailleur, un chemisier, des collants, des bottes, un foulard et des gants.
6. Bernard porte un complet, une chemise, une cravate, des socquettes et des chaussures.

E. La maison d'être. You will hear the story of a man's life, using verbs that take **être** as auxiliary verb in the **passé composé.** Write the number of each sentence by the spot on the drawing where the described action takes place.

1. Il est né.
2. Il est arrivé au monde.
3. Il est venu de l'hôpital.
4. Il est entré dans la maison.
5. Il est monté.
6. Il est resté.
7. Il est descendu.
8. Houp! Il est tombé.
9. Il est retourné de son voyage.
10. Il est revenu à la maison.
11. Il est rentré dans la maison.
12. Houp! Il est tombé encore une fois.
13. Il est devenu malade.
14. Il est mort.

F. Allons encore plus loin. You will hear a passage that expands on this chapter's vocabulary and grammar. Listen carefully as the passage is read twice. You may not understand every word, but you should be able to follow the story line. You will then hear a series of questions and possible answers. Based on your understanding of the story, circle the letter of the best answer to each question.

NARRATOR: Nicole entre dans une boutique.
NICOLE: Bonjour, madame.
VENDEUSE: Bonjour, mademoiselle.
NICOLE: Je désire une robe en coton.
VENDEUSE: Vous faites quelle taille?
NICOLE: Du 36.
VENDEUSE: Par ici, mademoiselle. Comme vous le voyez, nous avons un excellent choix. Quelle couleur préférez-vous?
NICOLE: Le bleu.
VENDEUSE: Ah, je regrette. Je ne trouve pas de robe bleue. Mais voici une robe verte, des gants en nylon, des bottes de cuir, des cardigans et des bas.
NICOLE: Mais...
VENDEUSE: Nous avons aussi des vestes, des blouses, des slips et des robes en soie.
NICOLE: Mais, vous n'y êtes pas. C'est une robe bleue...
NARRATOR: Une femme passe devant la boutique. La vendeuse voit qu'elle porte une robe bleue.
VENDEUSE: Ah, la voilà.
NARRATOR: Elle court hors de la boutique.
NICOLE: En voilà une femme bizarre.

1. Que désire Nicole?
   a. Une robe en soie.
   b. Une robe en coton.
   c. Une robe sur une colonne.

2. De quelle taille?
   a. Du 36.
   b. Du 42.
   c. Du 56.

3. Est-ce qu'il y a un excellent choix?
   a. Oui.
   b. Non.
   c. Peut-être.

4. Nicole veut une robe de quelle couleur?
   a. Verte.
   b. Bleue.
   c. Beige.

5. Est-ce que la vendeuse trouve une robe de cette couleur?
   a. Non.
   b. Oui.
   c. Peut-être.

6. Qu'est-ce que la vendeuse propose?
   a. Une robe de verre.
   b. Une robe verte.
   c. Une robe avec des vers.

7. Et quoi d'autre?
   a. Des gants en nylon.
   b. Des bottes de laine.
   c. Des bas bleus.

8. Qu'est-ce qui se passe?
   a. Une femme passe derrière la boutique.
   b. Une femme passe devant la banque.
   c. Une femme passe devant la boutique.

9. Que voit la vendeuse?
   a. Que la femme porte une robe en nylon.
   b. Que la femme porte une robe de soie.
   c. Que la femme porte une robe bleue.

10. Que fait la vendeuse?
    a. Elle mange un sandwich.
    b. Elle court hors de la boutique.
    c. Elle fait la cour.

11. Que dit Nicole?
    a. Que la vendeuse est jolie.
    b. Que la vendeuse est trop sérieuse.
    c. Que la vendeuse est bizarre.

This is the end of the taped activities for Chapter 8.

A. Scénario. Listen carefully to the conversation as Nicole teaches Robert how to ride a moped. You may not understand every word, but you should be able to follow the story line.

NICOLE: Voilà ta mob! Il est nécessaire d'en prendre soin. On met de l'essence dans le réservoir, et hop!
ROBERT: Et qu'est-ce que je fais après?
NICOLE: Tu es déjà monté à bicyclette, non?
ROBERT: Bien sûr, je suis monté à bicyclette.
NICOLE: Eh bien, c'est le même principe. La différence c'est que ce moteur va t'aider. Vas-y!
NARRATOR: Robert réussit.
NICOLE: Bravo! Ça y est! Tu as bien commencé ta première leçon. Tu n'es pas tombé. Attends, j'ai une idée: je vais prendre ma mob aussi et nous allons nous promener en ville ensemble. Tu vas voir des choses intéressantes.
ROBERT: J'en ai déjà beaucoup vu, tu sais.
NICOLE: Bon, bon! Avant de partir, n'oublie pas qu'on a toujours la priorité à droite. Ne perds jamais la tête! Et surtout, attention aux piétons, il y en a beaucoup. Tu leur laisses le passage. Comme mon père t'a dit, il faut savoir freiner. Ne t'aventure pas dans les rues sans avoir tous les papiers nécessaires au cas où tu es arrêté par un flic.

B. A vous maintenant! Listen again to the **scénario** and repeat during the pauses. Pay particular attention to pronunciation and intonation.

NICOLE: Voilà ta mob!// Il est nécessaire // d'en prendre soin.// On met de l'essence // dans le réservoir,// et hop!//
ROBERT: Et qu'est-ce que je fais après?//
NICOLE: Tu es déjà monté // à bicyclette, non?//
ROBERT: Bien sûr,// je suis monté à bicyclette.//
NICOLE: Eh bien,// c'est le même principe.// La différence // c'est que ce moteur va t'aider.// Vas-y!//
NARRATOR: Robert réussit.//
NICOLE: Bravo! Ça y est!// Tu as bien commencé // ta première leçon.// Tu n'es pas tombé.// Attends, j'ai une idée:// je vais prendre ma mob aussi // et nous allons // nous promener en ville ensemble.// Tu vas voir // des choses intéressantes.//
ROBERT: J'en ai déjà beaucoup vu,// tu sais.//
NICOLE: Bon, bon!// Avant de partir,// n'oublie pas qu'on a toujours // la priorité à droite.// Ne perds jamais la tête!// Et surtout,// attention aux piétons,// il y en a beaucoup.// Tu leur laisses le passage.// Comme mon père t'a dit,// il faut savoir freiner.// Ne t'aventure pas // dans les rues// sans avoir tous les papiers nécessaires // au cas où tu es arrêté // par un flic.//

C. Prononciation: Liaison. Listen to the discussion of liaison and repeat the key phrases during the pauses.

1. Liaison is obligatory between a subject pronoun and a verb. Listen and repeat.

   vous‿avez [z] — on‿a [n] — ils‿écoutent [z] — nous‿écoutons [z] — ont‿-ils [t] — prend‿-il [t]

2. Liaison is obligatory between an article and an adjective and the noun that follows. Listen and repeat.

   Les‿assiettes [z] — six‿étudiants [z] — mon‿enfant [n] — neuf‿heures [v]

   huit‿ans [t] — le grand‿hôtel [t] — ces‿autres‿étudiants [z] [z]

3. Liaison is obligatory between a one-syllable adverb or preposition and the following word. Listen and repeat.

   pour‿eux [r] — sans‿un sou [z] — avec‿elle [k] — dans‿une heure [z]

   tout‿heureux [t] — en‿hiver [n] — très‿amusant [z] — de temps‿en temps [z]

D. Les animaux et leur langage. You will hear the names of eight animals. Write the number of each animal under the appropriate picture. You will then hear eight sounds that French animals make. Write the letter of each sound under the appropriate picture.

1. un chat
2. un chien
3. une vache
4. un mouton
5. un coq
6. une poule
7. un canard
8. un âne

a. Hi-han!
b. Coin-coin!
c. Miaou!
d. Ouah! Ouah!
e. Cocorico!
f. Cot-cot-codec!
g. Meuh!
h. Bêêêêê!

E. Le corps humain. You will hear nine sentences about parts of the body. Write the number of each sentence next to the body part to which it refers.

1. Elle a un grand nez.
2. Elle a les cheveux courts.
3. Ses jambes sont musclées.
4. Ses yeux sont sensibles au soleil.
5. Elle a mal au coude.
6. Elle a deux pieds.
7. Elle ne porte pas de bague au doigt.
8. Ses genoux sont pliés.
9. Ses épaules ne sont pas couvertes.

F. Un matin typique. Christine's younger sister has just returned home after spending a week with Christine and her husband Christophe. She is describing their morning routine to her mother who is asking for specifics. Answer her mother's questions about which items they use for each activity. Choose from the list provided. Follow the model.

Modèle: D'abord, il se réveille. — Avec quoi?
Avec (k) un réveil.

1. Il se lave. — Avec quoi?
2. Il se rase. — Avec quoi?
3. Il se brosse les dents. — Avec quoi?
4. Ensuite, il se peigne. — Avec quoi?
5. Il s'habille. — Qu'est-ce qu'il met?
6. Il s'en va. — Comment?
7. Christine se douche. — Avec quoi?
8. Elle se lave les cheveux. — Avec quoi?
9. Elle se brosse les dents. — Avec quoi?
10. Elle se brosse les cheveux. — Avec quoi?
11. Elle se maquille. — Avec quoi?
12. Elle s'habille. — Qu'est-ce qu'elle met?

G. Y a-t-il un choix? A professor is addressing a group of students during the course of a field trip to the Musée Picasso. Decide in each case whether he's asking a question or giving a command and check the appropriate column.

1. Avez-vous de l'argent?
2. Avez-vous apporté des cahiers?
3. Allez-y!
4. Vous promenez-vous lentement?
5. Allons-nous voir des sculptures?
6. Regardez les tableaux là-bas!
7. Aimez-vous celui-ci?
8. Allons voir des sculptures dans le jardin!

9. Avez-vous aimé la visite?
10. Dépêchez-vous! Le musée va fermer.

H. En retard. When Marie calls Monique to find out why she's late for the party, Monique gives her all the details. Listen to each of Monique's statements and check the appropriate column to tell if she is talking about something she has already done (**passé**), something she is currently doing (**présent**), or something she will do in the future (**futur**).

1. J'ai pris une douche.
2. Je me suis lavé les cheveux.
3. Je me brosse les cheveux.
4. Je vais me brosser les dents.
5. Je me maquille.
6. Je vais m'habiller.
7. J'ai lavé mes nouveaux vêtements.

I. Allons encore plus loin. You will hear a passage that expands on this chapter's vocabulary and grammar. Listen carefully as the passage is read twice. You may not understand every word, but you should be able to follow the story line. You will then hear a series of questions and possible answers. Based on your understanding of the story, circle the letter of the best answer to each question.

Argan, dans la pièce de théâtre de Molière, *Le Malade imaginaire,* devient volontiers victime de plusieurs charlatans. Il dépense beaucoup d'argent pour des médicaments. Il veut marier sa fille Angélique avec le fils de son médecin, M. Purgon. Il pense ainsi qu'il aura chez lui «la source des remèdes qui lui sont nécessaires». L'oncle d'Angélique et sa domestique Toinette décident de rompre ce projet de mariage et de prouver à Argan que sa femme ne l'aime vraiment pas, qu'elle aime seulement son argent. A la fin de la pièce, Argan voit que sa femme ne l'aime pas et il permet à Angélique de se marier avec l'homme qu'elle aime, Cléante. Le frère d'Argan le convainc de devenir médecin lui-même.

1. Quel est le nom de la pièce de Molière?
   a. *Le Malade inventaire.*
   b. *Le Malade imaginé.*
   c. *Le Malade imaginaire.*

2. Quel est le problème d'Argan?
   a. Il devient victime.
   b. Il devient charlatan.
   c. Il devient médecin.

3. Pourquoi dépense-il beaucoup d'argent?
   a. Pour ses projets de mariage.

b. Pour des médicaments.
c. Pour trouver une femme.

4. Argan veut marier sa fille Angélique avec...
   a. le fils de son médecin.
   b. son médecin qui a un fils.
   c. le Malade imaginaire.

5. La femme d'Argan...
   a. aime le médecin.
   b. est toujours malade.
   c. aime l'argent.

6. Avec qui se marie Angélique?
   a. Avec le médecin qu'elle n'aime pas.
   b. Avec le fils du médecin qu'elle aime.
   c. Avec Cléante qu'elle aime.

7. A la fin, que fait Argan?
   a. Il devient médecin.
   b. Il convainc son frère de devenir médecin.
   c. Il voit que sa femme l'aime.

This is the end of the taped activities for Chapter 9.

A. Scénario. Listen carefully to the conversation as Nicole and Robert visit **la cathédrale** Saint-Etienne.

ROBERT: Quel grand bâtiment! Il est immense, énorme, gigantesque!
NICOLE: Tu t'es écrié comme moi la première fois que je l'ai vu. Te souviens-tu de son histoire?
ROBERT: Non!
NICOLE: C'est la cathédrale Saint-Etienne qui date du douzième et du treizième siècles. Te rends-tu compte? Elle est là depuis presque huit siècles. Elle est gothique et c'est la seule cathédrale avec cinq portails.
ROBERT: Je me demande si c'est le plus beau bâtiment de la ville.
NICOLE: C'est surtout le plus important. Elle contient aussi le plus grand nombre de vitraux de toutes les cathédrales.
ROBERT: Parle plus lentement, je te prie.
NICOLE: D'accord. Entrons! Tu y verras de véritables merveilles de la civilisation française.
ROBERT: Oui, je le sais, j'ai acheté ce livre qui décrit la cathédrale.
NICOLE: Pourquoi? Je suis là. Tu n'en as pas besoin maintenant. Donne-le-moi! Je t'apprendrai à l'apprécier. Tu l'as dit: je suis ton guide.
ROBERT: Tiens, prends-le! Mais n'oublie pas de me le rendre.

B. A vous maintenant! Listen again to the **scénario** and repeat during the pauses. Pay particular attention to pronunciation and intonation.

ROBERT: Quel grand bâtiment!// Il est immense,// énorme,// gigantesque!//
NICOLE: Tu t'es écrié // comme moi la première fois // que je l'ai vu.// Te souviens-tu de son histoire?//
ROBERT: Non!//
NICOLE: C'est la cathédrale Saint-Etienne // qui date du douzième // et du treizième siècles.// Te rends-tu compte?// Elle est là // depuis presque huit siècles.// Elle est gothique // et c'est la seule cathédrale // avec cinq portails.//
ROBERT: Je me demande // si c'est le plus beau bâtiment de la ville.//
NICOLE: C'est surtout // le plus important.// Elle contient aussi // le plus grand nombre de vitraux // de toutes les cathédrales.//
ROBERT: Parle plus lentement,// je te prie.//
NICOLE: D'accord.// Entrons!// Tu y verras de véritables merveilles // de la civilisation française.//
ROBERT: Oui, je le sais,// j'ai acheté ce livre // qui décrit la cathédrale.//
NICOLE: Pourquoi?// Je suis là.// Tu n'en as pas besoin maintenant.// Donne-le-moi!// Je t'apprendrai à l'apprécier.// Tu l'as dit:// je suis ton guide.//
ROBERT: Tiens, prends-le!// Mais n'oublie pas de me le rendre.//

C. Prononciation: Liaison. Listen to the discussion of liaison and repeat the key phrases during the pauses.

1. Liaison is absolutely forbidden after **et** and **cent**, and before **oui** and **onze**. Listen and repeat.

et // ils ont	ils sont forts et // intelligents	cent // un
cent // un	mais // oui, je suis là	le // onze avril

2. Liaison is absolutely forbidden before an aspirate **h**. Listen and repeat.

le // haut de la tour	le // héros de la tragédie	les // héros
le // huit mai	les // hors-d'œuvre	en // Hongrie

3. Liaison is absolutely forbidden when a noun precedes a verb or a singular adjective follows its nouns. Listen and repeat.

l'avion // arrive   l'hôtesse // apporte   Robert // écoute   l'étudiant // américain

4. Liaison is absolutely forbidden after an adverb not followed by **est-ce que**. Listen and repeat.

quand // est-il...?   comment // as-tu...?   combien // a-t-il...?

Except: comment‿allez-vous?

D. Les vacances internationales. You will hear about the vacations that different people are planning to take. You will hear the name of the city and the name of a tourist attraction that they will see. Draw a line to match the travelers with their destination. You will hear each cue twice. Follow the model.

Modèle: Marie visitera Rome où elle verra le Vatican.
Elle ira en Italie.

1. Nous visiterons Paris où nous verrons la tour Eiffel.
2. Marianne visitera Moscou où elle verra le Kremlin.
3. Vous visiterez Athènes où vous verrez l'Acropole.
4. Marc et Antoine visiteront Copenhague où ils verront le glypothèque Carlsberg.
5. Tu visiteras Bucarest où tu verras l'église du Curtea Veche.
6. Je visiterai Casablanca où je verrai Rick's Café Américain.
7. Ils visiteront Londres où ils verront Big Ben.
8. Pierre va à Lisbonne où il verra la statue de Corpus Christi et le Tage.

Now read the complete sentences that result from matching the columns during the pauses provided. You will hear the correct answers after each pause.

Modèle: *Marie ira en Italie.*

1. Nous irons à Paris.
2. Marianne ira dans la Communauté des états indépendants.
3. Vous irez en Grèce.
4. Marc et Annette iront au Danemark.
5. Tu iras en Roumanie.
6. J'irai au Maroc.
7. Ils iront en Angleterre.
8. Pierre ira au Portugal.

E. **Les rendez-vous à 2 h.** Several people are waiting for their friends in different locations around town. Listen to the speaker tell where each person is waiting and since when. Fill in the watches with the time each person arrived.

1. Jean est arrivé au cinéma à une heure et demie.
2. Marthe est arrivée à la bibliothèque à une heure et quart.
3. Sylvie est arrivée au théâtre à deux heures moins dix.
4. Chérie est arrivée au musée à une heure.
5. Pascal est arrivé au concert à deux heures moins le quart.
6. Jean-Luc et Yves sont arrivés au restaurant à une heure vingt.

Now, listen to the speaker repeat the times, check the watches and make sure that you filled in the time correctly. It is now 2 o'clock. Since all of these people had rendez-vous for two o'clock, say how long each person has been waiting. The first one will be done as a model.

1. Jean est arrivé au cinéma à une heure et demie.// *Il attend depuis une demi-heure.*
2. Marthe est arrivée à la bibliothèque à une heure et quart.// Elle attend depuis quarante-cinq minutes.
3. Sylvie est arrivée au théâtre à deux heures moins dix.// Elle attend depuis dix minutes.
4. Chérie est arrivée au musée à une heure.// Elle attend depuis une heure.
5. Pascal est arrivé au concert à deux heures moins le quart.// Il attend depuis un quart d'heure. *OR:* Il attend depuis quinze minutes.
6. Jean-Luc et Yves sont arrivés au restaurant à une heure vingt.// Ils attendent depuis quarante minutes.

F. **Allons encore plus loin.** You will hear a passage that expands on this chapter's vocabulary and grammar. Listen carefully as the passage is read twice. You may not understand every word, but you should be able to follow the story line. You will then hear a series of questions and possible answers. Based on your understanding of the story, circle the letter of the best answer to each question.

Dans son livre *Notre-Dame de Paris*, Victor Hugo raconte l'histoire de Quasimodo. Quasimodo est un bossu qui n'est pas trop beau. Il habite dans la cathédrale où il sonne les cloches. Esmeralda est une jolie femme de seize ans. Claude Frollo est mauvais: il aime Esmeralda et la fait kidnapper par Quasimodo. Quasimodo tombe amoureux d'elle. Le beau capitaine Phébus la libère. Ils s'aiment. Frollo tue Phébus et laisse arrêter Esmeralda qu'on accuse d'assassinat. A la fin, Esmeralda est pendue. Quasimodo jette Frollo du haut de la cathédrale. Après, Quasimodo va mourir sur le corps de la belle Esmeralda.

1. Qui a écrit l'histoire de Quasimodo?
   a. Victor Hughes.
   b. Victor Hugo.
   c. Victor Shugrue.

2. L'action se passe où?
   a. Dans Notre-Dame de Paris.
   b. Dans Notre-Dame de Rockne.
   c. Dans Notre-Dame de Patrie.

3. Voici une description de Quasimodo:
   a. Beau et pas trop bossu.
   b. Bossu et pas trop beau.
   c. Bossu et pas trop bizarre.

4. Dans la cathédrale, Quasimodo...
   a. sonne la sonnerie.
   b. sonne les cloches.
   c. donne les cloches.

5. Voici une description d'Esmeralda:
   a. Une jolie jeune femme de six ans.
   b. Une jolie jeune femme de soixante ans.
   c. Une jolie jeune femme de seize ans.

6. Voici une description de Claude Frollo:
   a. Il est mauvais et il aime Quasimodo.
   b. Il est gentil et il aime Esmeralda.
   c. Il est mauvais et il aime Esmeralda.

7. Voici une description de Phébus:
   a. Il est beau et il libère Quasimodo.
   b. Il est beau et il libère Esmeralda.
   c. Il est beau et il aime Frollo.

8. Que fait Frollo?
   a. Il tue Esmeralda et fait arrêter Quasimodo.
   b. Il tue Phébus et fait arrêter Esmeralda.
   c. Il tue Phébus et laisse arrêter Esmeralda.

9. Que fait Quasimodo?
   a. Il jette Frollo de la cathédrale.
   b. Il jette Frollo de la fenêtre.
   c. Il jette Frollo dans une corbeille.

10. Que fait Quasimodo?
   a. Il va mourir sur le corps d'Esmeralda.
   b. Il va mourir sur le corps de Frollo.
   c. Il va mourir sur le corps de Phébus.

This is the end of the taped activities for Chapter 10.

A. Scénario. Listen carefully to the conversations surrounding an accident. You may not understand every word, but you should be able to follow the story line.

NARRATOR: Nicole et Robert roulent en mobylette. Nicole veut lui faire connaître la ville. Tout d'un coup, ils voient deux voitures qui se tamponnent.

PREMIER CHAUFFEUR: (*il saute de sa voiture, tout en gesticulant*) Espèce d'imbécile, tu ne peux pas regarder où tu vas? Où as-tu trouvé ton permis de conduire? Dans une pochette-surprise?

DEUXIEME CHAUFFEUR: (*même jeu*) C'est toi, crétin, qui es aveugle. Tu ne vois pas clair? Tu as brûlé un feu! Tu as enfoncé ma porte!

NARRATOR: Un agent de police arrive sur la scène.

AGENT DE POLICE: Ça suffit! Montrez-moi vos papiers et cessez de hurler comme des fous! Expliquez-moi vos dégâts et votre histoire!

NICOLE: S'ils n'ont pas de papiers, il va les amener au commissariat de police et ils vont perdre des heures.

ROBERT: Regarde! Ils ont peur du flic. Maintenant, ils ne se disputent plus.

AGENT DE POLICE: Cherchez vos constats à l'amiable!

ROBERT: (*chuchotant à Nicole*) Amiable? Tout à l'heure, ils étaient sur le point de se couper la gorge. Les Français sont plus difficiles à comprendre que les Américains.

NICOLE: Attends! Tu ne nous connais pas encore!

B. A vous maintenant! Listen again to the **scénario** and repeat during the pauses. Pay particular attention to pronunciation and intonation.

NARRATOR: Nicole et Robert roulent // en mobylette.// Nicole veut lui faire connaître la ville.// Tout d'un coup,// ils voient deux voitures // qui se tamponnent.//

PREMIER CHAUFFEUR: (*il saute de sa voiture, tout en gesticulant*) Espèce d'imbécile,// tu ne peux pas regarder // où tu vas?// Où as-tu trouvé // ton permis de conduire?// Dans une pochette-surprise?//

DEUXIEME CHAUFFEUR: (*même jeu*) C'est toi, crétin,// qui es aveugle.// Tu ne vois pas clair?// Tu as brûlé un feu!// Tu as enfoncé ma porte!//

NARRATOR: Un agent de police arrive // sur la scène.//

AGENT DE POLICE: Ça suffit!// Montrez-moi vos papiers // et cessez de hurler // comme des fous!// Expliquez-moi vos dégâts // et votre histoire!//

NICOLE: S'ils n'ont pas de papiers,// il va les amener // au commissariat de police // et ils vont perdre // des heures.//

ROBERT: Regarde!// Ils ont peur du flic.// Maintenant,// ils ne se disputent plus.//

AGENT DE POLICE: Cherchez vos constats // à l'amiable!//

ROBERT: (*chuchotant à Nicole*) Amiable?// Tout à l'heure,// ils étaient sur le point // de se couper la gorge.// Les Français sont plus difficiles // à comprendre // que les Américains.//

NICOLE: Attends!// Tu ne nous connais pas encore!//

C. **Prononciation:** **REVIEW OF ALL SIXTEEN VOWEL SOUNDS.** Listen carefully and note the vowel combinations repeated as directed during the pauses.

Orals

1. [a] table, la, avocat, gare, article, art, chat, cheval; moi, toi, loi, fois, boîte, fe(m)me.

2. [ɑ] pas, passer, classe, tasse; pâté, âge; trois, bois

3. [e] thé, école, métier, été, dîner, nez, pied, clef; j'ai

4. [ɛ] père, mère, frère; tête, fête, fenêtre, même; lait, je savais; terre, verre, neige

5. [i] si, rire, ici, il finit, lit, six, vie

6. [o] pot, dos, trop, le nôtre, eau, beau, chapeau, veau, chaud

7. [ɔ] robe, notre, homme, comme, joli, pomme, Paul, album

8. [u] vous, cou, toujours, écouter, nous, tout, bout, où, ou, août

Nasals

1. [œ̃] un, lundi, brun, chacun

2. [õ] [ɔ̃] on, bon, bonté, non, nom, oncle, compter

3. [ɛ̃] vin, vingt, impossible; pain, main, faim; il peint

4. [ɑ̃] blanc, an, lampe, lent, Jean, anglais, dent, temps, sans, chambre

Compound vowels

1. [ə] je, me, te, se, ce, de, venir, demain, demander

2. [y] tu, sur, rue, vu, statue, vendu

3. [ɸ] feu, peu, œufs, vieux, bleu, nombreux, deux

4. [œ] cœur, peur, sœur, œuf, fleur

D. **Assez ou pas assez?** Look at the pictures and notice how much each item costs. You will hear what eight people want to buy and how much money each one has. Decide whether or not each person has enough money and check the appropriate column. Follow the models.

Modèles: Serge veut acheter un magazine. Il a 2 €.
Il a assez d'argent.
Michel veut acheter un disque. Il a 21 €.
Il n'a pas assez d'argent.

1. Catherine veut acheter un chat. Elle a 200 €.
2. Georges veut acheter un Coca. Il a 10 €.
3. Madeleine veut acheter du shampoing. Elle a 7 €.
4. Yvette veut acheter un livre. Elle a 15 €.
5. Marc veut acheter un magazine. Il a 9 €.
6. Robert veut acheter un thé. Il a 3 €.
7. Marianne veut acheter un chat et un disque. Elle a 300 €.
8. Jean-Michel veut acheter un livre et un Coca. Il a 12 €.

E. Faire des achats. Anne made a list before she went shopping with her friend Michèle, but she ended up buying more than she had intended. Listen to each statement and compare Anne's list to her receipt. Then check **vrai** if the statement is true or **faux** if it is false.

1. Anne a acheté trop de pulls.
2. Anne a acheté peu de stylos.
3. Anne a acheté assez de disques.
4. Anne a acheté peu de livres.
5. Anne a acheté pas mal de robes.

Now compare Anne's receipt with Michèle's and decide if the following statements are true **(vrai)** or false **(faux)**.

6. Anne a acheté autant de livres que Michèle.
7. Anne a acheté plus de disques que Michèle.
8. Michèle a acheté plus de robes qu'Anne.
9. Michèle a acheté moins de pulls qu'Anne.
10. Anne a acheté autant de stylos que Michèle.

F. Un petit poème. Repeat this poem to help you remember most of the adjectives that precede the noun. (The opposites of these adjectives also precede the noun.)

petit grand - gros
vilain joli beau
autre long
mauvais bon
jeune vieux nouveaux

G. Soyez logique! You will hear descriptions of ten people's likes and dislikes. Using that information, decide which type of item or animal each is buying. Then circle the adjective that most logically completes each sentence and cross out the one that does not work. Follow the model.

Modèle: Il aime les voitures très bon marché.
Il achète une (vieille) voiture (chère).

1. Nous aimons les pommes de terre avec beaucoup de calories.
2. Elle adore le chocolat.
3. Vous aimez les immenses maisons.
4. Je suis connaisseur de champagne.
5. Tu aimes les chiens qui peuvent habiter dans un appartement.
6. Nous aimons les chiens qui peuvent protéger notre maison et faire peur aux étrangers.
7. Vous aimez les chats qui ne font pas beaucoup de bruit.
8. Il aime les chats qui ne sont pas gentils.
9. Vous aimez les fleurs qui sont agréables aux yeux.
10. Tu aimes les fromages doux qui n'ont pas de goût fort.

H. Allons encore plus loin. You will hear a passage that expands on this chapter's vocabulary and grammar. Listen carefully as the passage is read twice. You may not understand every word, but you should be able to follow the story line. You will then hear a series of questions and possible answers. Based on your understanding of the story, circle the letter of the best answer to each question.

Les Misérables est un long roman. Jean Valjean a de nombreuses aventures. L'inspecteur Javert le poursuit, parce qu'il s'est évadé de prison. Jean Valjean promet de s'occuper de l'enfant d'une femme malheureuse, la petite Cosette, et ils vont à Paris. L'inspecteur Javert le recherche partout. Valjean et Cosette trouvent asile dans un couvent. Quelques années plus tard, Cosette et un jeune homme nommé Marius tombent amoureux l'un de l'autre. Un peu après, Jean Valjean trouve un billet dans lequel il apprend que les jeunes gens s'aiment. Durant une bataille à Paris, Valjean sauve Marius qui est blessé. Marius guérit et se marie avec Cosette. Valjean révèle sa vraie identité et s'en va. A la fin, Valjean meurt parce qu'il n'a plus Cosette auprès de lui.

1. Qu'est-ce que c'est que *Les Misérables*?
   a. *Les Misérables* habitent l'Italie.
   b. *Les Misérables* sont grands.
   c. *Les Misérables* est un long roman.

2. Qu'est-ce qu'il a, Jean Valjean?
   a. Jean Valjean connaît plusieurs demoiselles.
   b. Jean Valjean a des aventures.
   c. Jean Valjean manque le train.

3. Que fait l'inspecteur Javert?
   a. L'inspecteur Javert le poursuit.
   b. L'inspecteur Javert est pour sa suite.
   c. L'inspecteur Javert est triste.

4. Qui Jean Valjean prend-il avec lui?
   a. Valjean prend Cosette avec lui.

b. Valjean prend une femme malheureuse avec lui.
c. Valjean prend un cheval avec lui.

5. Qui est Cosette?
   a. On entend de la musique sur une Cosette.
   b. Cosette est l'enfant d'une femme infortunée.
   c. Cosette est la fille de Javert.

6. Qu'est-ce qu'ils font dans le couvent?
   a. Valjean devient prêtre.
   b. Cosette devient nonne.
   c. Ils trouvent asile dans un couvent.

7. Que font Cosette et Marius?
   a. Cosette est plus âgée que Marius?
   b. Cosette et Marius tombent amoureux de Valjean.
   c. Cosette et Marius tombent amoureux l'un de l'autre.

8. Quelle est l'histoire du billet?
   a. Valjean trouve un billet pour le train.
   b. Un billet est un ticket.
   c. Valjean trouve un billet.

9. Qu'est-ce que Valjean fait à la guerre?
   a. Valjean fait la guerre à Paris.
   b. Valjean sauve Marius qui est blessé.
   c. Valjean aime Paris.

10. Que fait Marius?
   a. Marius blesse Valjean.
   b. Marius est blessé.
   c. Marius guérit Cosette.

11. Que font Marius et Cosette quand Marius est guéri?
   a. Marius et Cosette se marient.
   b. Marius et Cosette s'enfuient.
   c. Marius et Cosette se nourrissent.

12. Pourquoi meurt-il, Valjean?
   a. Valjean meurt parce qu'il est malade.
   b. Valjean meurt parce qu'il est blessé.
   c. Valjean meurt parce que Cosette n'est plus avec lui.

This is the end of the taped activities for Chapter 11.

A. Scénario. Listen carefully to the discussion as Robert and the Fourchet family await dinner. You may not understand every word, but you should be able to follow the story line.

NARRATOR: M. Fourchet est de retour. Nicole et Robert mettent la table.
M. FOURCHET: On va voir les nouvelles. Tu aimes la télé, Robert?
ROBERT: Moi, je la regarde de temps en temps chez nous.
M. FOURCHET: Des six chaînes que nous avons ici en France, c'est la première que je préfère. Il est huit heures. C'est maintenant l'heure des informations.
NARRATOR: M. Fourchet regarde le journal parlé. Mme Fourchet parle aux enfants.
MME FOURCHET: Qu'avez-vous fait aujourd'hui?
ROBERT: Nous sommes passés par le palais Jacques-Cœur. Ensuite, nous sommes allés à la cathédrale.
NICOLE: Oui, et là, nous avons vu un accident.
MME FOURCHET: Pas grave, j'espère.
NICOLE: Non, mais Robert a pu voir les Français en action. Après, je lui ai servi de guide dans la cathédrale.
ROBERT: Tiens, tu as oublié de me rendre mon livre. Rends-le-moi, s'il te plaît!
NICOLE: Je ne te l'ai pas rendu? Ah, non, je l'ai mis sur la table. Le voici.
M. FOURCHET: Regardez! On parle de Chambord. J'ai une bonne idée. Je vous y conduirai tous dimanche. Robert verra le spectacle son et lumière à Chambord.

B. A vous maintenant! Listen again to the **scénario** and repeat during the pauses. Pay particular attention to pronunciation and intonation.

NARRATOR: M. Fourchet est de retour.// Nicole et Robert mettent la table.//
M. FOURCHET: On va voir les nouvelles.// Tu aimes la télé, Robert?//
ROBERT: Moi, je la regarde // de temps en temps chez nous.//
M. FOURCHET: Des six chaînes // que nous avons ici en France,// c'est la première que je préfère.// Il est huit heures.// C'est maintenant // l'heure des informations.//
NARRATOR: M. Fourchet regarde le journal parlé.// Mme Fourchet parle aux enfants.//
MME FOURCHET: Qu'avez-vous fait aujourd'hui?//
ROBERT: Nous sommes passés // par le palais Jacques-Cœur.// Ensuite, nous sommes allés // à la cathédrale.//
NICOLE: Oui, et là, nous avons vu un accident.//
MME FOURCHET: Pas grave, j'espère.//
NICOLE: Non, mais Robert a pu voir // les Français en action.// Après, je lui ai servi de guide // dans la cathédrale.//

ROBERT: Tiens, tu as oublié // de me rendre mon livre.// Rends-le-moi, s'il te plaît!//

NICOLE: Je ne te l'ai pas rendu?// Ah, non, je l'ai mis sur la table.// Le voici.//

M. FOURCHET: Regardez!// On parle de Chambord.// J'ai une bonne idée.// Je vous y conduirai tous dimanche.// Robert verra le spectacle son et lumière à Chambord.//

C. **On fait ça avec quoi?** You will hear descriptions of how six items are used. Write the letter of the item you would use for each activity.

1. On prend des photos avec ça.
2. C'est l'appareil le plus moderne pour bien écouter la musique.
3. Si on veut faire une vidéo d'un événement spécial, on utilise ça.
4. Avec cet appareil on peut écouter de la musique sans déranger personne.
5. On peut regarder des vidéos à la télé avec cet appareil.
6. On utilise ça pour enregistrer des films de la télévision.

D. **Comment sont-ils?** You will hear descriptions of eight people. For each description, change the adjective in the first sentence into an adverb that will appropriately complete the second sentence. Say your answer during the pause. You will then hear the correct answer. Follow the model.

Modèle: Marc est libre.
Il parle librement.

1. Nancy est rapide.
   Elle marche rapidement.
2. Christian est consciencieux.
   Il travaille consciencieusement.
3. Annette est précise.
   Elle raconte son histoire précisément.
4. Jean-Luc est lent.
   Il court lentement.
5. Anne est prudente.
   Elle décide prudemment.
6. Nous sommes actifs.
   Nous vivons activement.
7. Michèle est patiente.
   Elle attend patiemment.
8. Henri est gentil.
   Il sourit gentiment.

E. **Allons encore plus loin.** You will hear a passage that expands on this chapter's vocabulary and grammar. Listen carefully as the passage is read twice. You may not understand every word, but you should be able to follow the story line. You will then hear a series of questions and possible answers. Based on your understanding of the story, circle the letter of the best answer to each question.

Un dimanche en Provence

La vie est très calme. Les enfants jouent au football. Le matin, les femmes vont à la messe revêtues de leurs beaux vêtements du dimanche pendant que les hommes sont au café. Ils prennent l'apéritif et après ils jouent à la pétanque — un jeu de boules où tout le monde donne son opinion — sous les arbres de la place du village. On prend un gros repas le dimanche à midi avec des hors-d'œuvre, le gigot traditionnel, des gâteaux et beaucoup de vin. Après, tout le monde va assister au match de football. Vers cinq heures, on va aux arènes pour voir les courses de taureaux. On finit la journée par un bal à la fraîcheur.

1. La vie en Provence est...
   a. très calme.
   b. très palme.
   c. très normale.

2. Les enfants jouent...
   a. aux boules.
   b. au football.
   c. au babyfoot.

3. Qu'est-ce qui se passe le matin?
   a. Les femmes vont à la messe.
   b. Les femmes vont à la presse.
   c. Les femmes vont à la crèche.

4. Que font les hommes?
   a. Ils prennent l'apéritif.
   b. Ils prennent de l'aspirine.
   c. Ils prennent l'article.

5. Que font-ils après?
   a. Ils jouent aux pétards.
   b. Ils jouent à la pétanque.
   c. Ils jouent à la banque.

6. Que font les gens durant le jeu?
   a. Tout le monde fume des cigares.
   b. Tout le monde donne un oignon.
   c. Tout le monde donne son opinion.

7. Où joue-t-on à la pétanque d'habitude?
   a. Sous les arbres du centre du village.
   b. Sous les arbres de la place du village.
   c. Sur les arbres de la place du village.

8. Qu'est-ce qu'on sert tout de suite après les hors-d'œuvre?
   a. Le gigot conventionnel.

b. Le gigot traditionnel.
c. Le gigot banal.

9. Qu'est-ce qu'on fait le dimanche après-midi?
   a. On allume des cigarettes.
   b. On va au match.
   c. On joue au catch.

10. Qu'est-ce qu'on fait vers cinq heures?
    a. On va aux arènes pour voir les bureaux.
    b. On va aux arènes pour voir les carreaux.
    c. On va aux arènes pour voir les taureaux.

11. Comment finit-on la journée?
    a. Par un bal à la fraîcheur.
    b. Par un bal à la française.
    c. Par un bal à la framboise.

This is the end of the taped activities for Chapter 12.

A. Scénario. Listen carefully as Nicole and Madame Fourchet give Robert some advice on letter writing. You may not understand every word, but you should be able to follow the story line.

NICOLE: Je vois que la lettre que tu as écrite à ta mère est toujours là sur ton bureau. Dis donc, Robert, qu'est-ce que tu lui racontes?

ROBERT: Eh bien, je lui ai dit que ton père nous a conduits à la campagne dimanche dernier, que tu étais la plus jolie de toutes les filles que j'ai rencontrées en France, malheureusement que tu parlais trop vite que...

NICOLE: Oh, là, là! Il n'y a rien d'intéressant là-dedans. Ta lettre est vraiment rasoir. Si tu lui parlais plutôt de la cuisine française? Tu peux lui dire que tu aimes mieux le veau que le boudin et que tu aimes moins la tête de veau que le pâté et que tu as refusé de manger du cheval et du lapin.

MME FOURCHET: Dis-lui aussi que tout le monde ici te félicite parce que tu fais des progrès remarquables en français.

NICOLE: Oui, et mets-lui une de ces belles photos de la cathédrale que tu aimes tant. Ou parle-lui de l'accident que nous avons vu.

ROBERT: Si tu sais mieux que moi tout ce qu'il faut dire, veux-tu lui écrire cette lettre pour moi? Tu m'embêtes!

NICOLE: Ne te fâche pas! Je voulais t'aider. Après ceci, n'attends plus pour la finir et la mettre à la boîte.

B. A vous maintenant! Listen again to the **scénario** and repeat during the pauses. Pay particular attention to pronunciation and intonation.

NICOLE: Je vois que la lettre // que tu as écrite à ta mère // est toujours là sur ton bureau.// Dis donc, Robert,// qu'est-ce que tu lui racontes?//

ROBERT: Eh bien,// je lui ai dit // que ton père nous a conduits// à la campagne dimanche dernier,// que tu étais la plus jolie // de toutes les filles // que j'ai rencontrées en France,// malheureusement que tu parlais trop vite que...//

NICOLE: Oh, là, là!// Il n'y a rien d'intéressant là-dedans.// Ta lettre est vraiment rasoir.// Si tu lui parlais plutôt // de la cuisine française?// Tu peux lui dire // que tu aimes mieux // le veau que le boudin // et que tu aimes moins // la tête de veau que le pâté // et que tu as refusé de manger // du cheval et du lapin.//

MME FOURCHET: Dis-lui aussi // que tout le monde ici te félicite // parce que tu fais des progrès remarquables en français.//

NICOLE: Oui, et mets-lui une de ces belles photos // de la cathédrale que tu aimes tant.// Ou parle-lui de l'accident // que nous avons vu.//

ROBERT: Si tu sais mieux // que moi // tout ce qu'il faut dire,// veux-tu lui écrire cette lettre pour moi?// Tu m'embêtes!//

NICOLE: Ne te fâche pas!// Je voulais t'aider.// Après ceci,// n'attends plus pour la finir // et la mettre à la boîte.//

C. La voiture. You will hear a series of sentences about parts of a car. Write the number of each sentence next to the car part to which it refers.

1. J'ai un pneu à plat.
2. Quand il pleut, on fait marcher les essuie-glaces.
3. Les pare-chocs protègent un peu la voiture.
4. On met les valises dans la malle.
5. Il est essentiel d'allumer les phares quand il fait nuit.
6. Pour vérifier le niveau d'huile, il faut ouvrir le capot.
7. Dans le rétroviseur, on voit la voiture qui est derrière.
8. On doit souvent nettoyer le pare-brise.

D. Passé composé ou imparfait? Listen as Patrick describes a recent shopping trip, paying particular attention to the verb tenses. If a sentence describes an ongoing or incompleted action, check **imparfait**; if it expresses a completed action, check **passé composé**.

1. Mon ami m'a invité à une boum.
2. C'était pour l'anniversaire de notre amie Céleste.
3. J'ai voulu acheter un cadeau.
4. Il y avait beaucoup de monde au centre commercial.
5. Je suis entré dans une excellente boutique.
6. Il y avait pas mal de bonnes choses pour Céleste.
7. J'ai choisi un bracelet africain et un beau tee-shirt noir.
8. J'ai payé avec une carte de crédit.
9. J'étais très content de mon achat.

E. Interruptions. You will hear a series of sentences that describe what was going on when something else happened. For each sentence, circle the infinitive of the verb that expresses the action that was interrupted.

1. Nous regardions la télé quand papa est rentré.
2. Vous chantiez lorsque le téléphone a sonné.
3. Quand nous avons vu Bruno, il faisait des achats en ville.
4. Les enfants dormaient quand leurs parents sont sortis.
5. Je l'ai appelé lorsqu'il se rasait.
6. Ma mère est arrivée lorsque je préparais le dîner.

F. Les comparaisons. Study the table to see what Nathalie, Marguerite, and Joseph did during the month-long winter break and note how many times each person did each thing. You will then hear six questions about their activities. Circle the best answer to each question.

1. Qui a conduit le mieux de tous les étudiants?
2. Qui est allé au cinéma le plus souvent?
3. Qui a rendu visite à des amis le moins souvent?
4. Qui a écrit des lettres plus souvent que Nathalie?
5. Qui a téléphoné le moins souvent à des parents?
6. Qui a moins bien conduit, Marguerite ou Joseph?

G. Allons encore plus loin. You will hear a passage that expands on this chapter's vocabulary and grammar. Listen carefully as the passage is read twice. You may not understand every word, but you should be able to follow the story line. You will then hear a series of questions and possible answers. Based on your understanding of the story, circle the letter of the best answer to each question.

Le dix-huitième siècle a donné naissance à de nombreuses œuvres littéraires, incorporant tous les genres, c'est-à-dire le roman, le drame et la poésie. Parmi les œuvres importantes de cette époque, on peut citer le roman consistant de lettres, ou le roman épistolaire. Par une curieuse coïncidence, les quatre romans épistolaires du siècle sont séparés par des intervalles d'à peu près vingt ans: Montesquieu a écrit *Les Lettres persanes* en 1721; *Pamela* (ou *La Vertu récompensée*) de l'auteur anglais Richardson en 1740; *La Nouvelle Héloïse* (ou *Julie et La Nouvelle Héloïse*) de Jean-Jacques Rousseau en 1761 et *Les Liaisons dangereuses* de Laclos en 1782.

1. En quoi est-ce que le dix-huitième siècle a été riche?
   a. En laitue.
   b. En lettres.
   c. En littérature.

2. Quelle sorte de roman peut-on citer parmi les œuvres importantes?
   a. Les œuvres importantes parlent de pastrami.
   b. Les œuvres importantes parlent de romains.
   c. Les œuvres importantes sont des romans épistolaires.

3. De quoi est fait le roman épistolaire?
   a. Un roman épistolaire traite de pistoles.
   b. Un roman épistolaire est fait de lettres.
   c. Un roman épistolaire est fait de laitue.

4. Par quoi les quatre romans sont-ils séparés?
   a. Les quatre romans sont séparés par des vallées.
   b. Les quatre romans sont séparés par du vin.
   c. Les quatre romans sont séparés par des périodes de vingt ans.

5. Qu'est-ce que Montesquieu a écrit?
   a. Montesquieu a écrit *Les Lettres parisiennes.*
   b. Montesquieu a écrit *Les Lettres imparfaites.*
   c. Montesquieu a écrit *Les Lettres persanes.*

6. Qu'est-ce que c'est que *Pamela*?
   a. *Pamela* est le nom de l'auteur anglais.
   b. *Pamela* est le nom d'un roman.
   c. *Pamela* est une femme bizarre.

7. Quand Rousseau a-t-il écrit *La Nouvelle Héloïse*?
   a. Rousseau a écrit *La Nouvelle Héloïse* en 1761.
   b. Rousseau a écrit *La Nouvelle Héloïse* en 1641.
   c. Rousseau a écrit *La Nouvelle Héloïse* en 1731.

8. Qui a écrit *Les Liaisons dangereuses*?
   a. Glenn Close a écrit *Les Liaisons dangereuses*.
   b. Laclos a écrit *Les Liaisons dangereuses*.
   c. Laclos a écrit *Les Liaisons ténébreuses*.

This is the end of the taped activities for Chapter 13.

A. Scénario. Listen to the conversations as Henry, Robert, Nicole, and Marguerite leave the theater and arrive at their hotel. You may not understand every word, but you should be able to follow the story line.

NARRATOR: Les quatre jeunes gens sortent du théâtre où ils ont vu *la Cantatrice chauve*. Ils sont enthousiasmés. Ils se dirigent vers leur hôtel.
HENRY: Nous avons eu de la chance d'avoir lu un passage de cette pièce. Cela nous a aidés à mieux comprendre la pensée de Ionesco.
ROBERT: Oui, c'est vrai. J'ai pu comprendre le dialogue qu'il a écrit et la raison pour les pièces qu'il a faites. On ne pense pas quand on parle et on n'écoute pas les autres. Ah! Voilà notre hôtel. Entrons!
NARRATOR: A la réception...
LA PATRONNE: Bonsoir, messieurs dames. Vous désirez?
NICOLE: Nous avons deux chambres réservées.
LA PATRONNE: Oui. A quel nom, s'il vous plaît?
NICOLE: Fourchet. Olivier Fourchet. C'est lui qui a fait la réservation.
LA PATRONNE: Attendez un instant. Oui. C'est ça, deux chambres pour quatre personnes, pour une nuit, avec douches. Les toilettes sont sur le palier. Cela fera cent quatre-vingts francs pour chaque chambre. Le petit déjeuner est compris. Vous avez les chambres 42 et 44. Voici les clefs. Bonsoir, messieurs dames.
NARRATOR: Arrivés au quatrième étage, les jeunes gens se séparent et se disent bonne nuit.
MARGUERITE: Nicole, as-tu pris une serviette?
NICOLE: Non, je défais mon sac de voyage. Pourquoi?
MARGUERITE: Je n'en trouve qu'une.
NICOLE: Je vais téléphoner pour qu'on nous en apporte une autre. Allô! madame. Je suis dans la chambre numéro 42. Il nous manque une serviette. Serait-il possible d'en avoir une autre? Merci d'avance. Bonsoir, madame. C'est fait. On va nous en monter une tout de suite.

B. A vous maintenant! Listen again to the **scénario** and repeat during the pauses. Pay particular attention to pronunciation and intonation.

NARRATOR: Les quatre jeunes gens sortent du théâtre // où ils ont vu *la Cantatrice chauve*.// Ils sont enthousiasmés.// Ils se dirigent vers leur hôtel.//
HENRY: Nous avons eu de la chance // d'avoir lu un passage de cette pièce.// Cela nous a aidés à mieux comprendre // la pensée de Ionesco.//
ROBERT: Oui, c'est vrai.// J'ai pu comprendre // le dialogue qu'il a écrit // et la raison pour les pièces // qu'il a faites.// On ne pense pas // quand on parle // et on n'écoute pas les autres.// Ah! Voilà notre hôtel.// Entrons!//
NARRATOR: A la réception... //

LA PATRONNE: Bonsoir, messieurs dames.// Vous désirez?//
NICOLE: Nous avons deux chambres réservées.//
LA PATRONNE: Oui. A quel nom,// s'il vous plaît?//
NICOLE: Fourchet. Olivier Fourchet.// C'est lui qui a fait la réservation.//
LA PATRONNE: Attendez un instant.// Oui. C'est ça,// deux chambres pour quatre personnes,// pour une nuit,// avec douches.// Les toilettes sont sur le palier.// Cela fera cent quatre-vingts francs // pour chaque chambre.// Le petit déjeuner est compris.// Vous avez les chambres 42 et 44.// Voici les clefs.// Bonsoir, messieurs dames.//
NARRATOR: Arrivés au quatrième étage,// les jeunes gens se séparent // et se disent bonne nuit.//
MARGUERITE: Nicole, as-tu pris une serviette?//
NICOLE: Non, je défais mon sac de voyage.// Pourquoi?//
MARGUERITE: Je n'en trouve qu'une.//
NICOLE: Je vais téléphoner // pour qu'on nous en apporte une autre.// Allô! madame.// Je suis dans la chambre numéro 42.// Il nous manque une serviette.// Serait-il possible // d'en avoir une autre?// Merci d'avance.// Bonsoir, madame.// C'est fait.// On va nous en monter une // tout de suite.//

C. On cherche un hôtel. Look over the descriptions of the three hotels. You will hear ten statements describing what people are looking for in a hotel. Listen carefully to each statement. Then determine which hotels meet that requirement and check the appropriate columns. (In some cases, there may be only one hotel that meets the requirement; in others, there will be more than one.)

1. Je cherche un hôtel avec un bon restaurant.
2. Moi, je voudrais une chambre avec douche.
3. Nous cherchons un hôtel avec petit déjeuner compris.
4. Nous voudrions trouver un hôtel de grand luxe.
5. Nous cherchons une situation tranquille.
6. Il faut que nous ayons une chambre non fumeur.
7. Il faut avoir du parking.
8. Nous avons besoin d'un téléphone dans la chambre.
9. Est-ce qu'il y a une piscine couverte?
10. Nous voudrions un hôtel avec ascenseur.

D. Allons encore plus loin. You will hear a passage that expands on this chapter's vocabulary and grammar. Listen carefully as the passage is read twice. You may not understand every word, but you should be able to follow the story line. You will then hear a series of questions and possible answers. Based on your understanding of the story, circle the letter of the best answer to each question.

Le salon

Au dix-huitième siècle, le salon était un lieu où les gens de lettres et les philosophes se retrouvaient pour rapporter les dernières nouvelles et en discuter.

Parmi ces gens, il y avait Montesquieu, un grand penseur et écrivain. Montesquieu fréquentait les salons et faisait des observations sur tout ce qu'il y voyait. Il a défini le salon comme un endroit où se réunissaient les «trompés» (les gens qui sont trompés), les trompeurs (ceux qui trompent les gens) et les trompettes (les gens qui font circuler des rumeurs).

1. Où se réunissaient les gens de lettres et les philosophes?
   a. Dans une salle à manger.
   b. Dans un salon.
   c. Dans un garage.

2. Qu'est-ce qu'ils y faisaient?
   a. Ils discutaient d'argent.
   b. Ils discutaient et échangeaient des romans.
   c. Ils discutaient des dernières nouvelles.

3. Qui se trouvait parmi eux?
   a. Un grand penseur et écrivain.
   b. Un grand pianiste et écrivassier.
   c. Un grand premier et étranger.

4. Comment s'appelait-il?
   a. Montesquieu.
   b. Montesqueue.
   c. Montesque.

5. Qu'est-ce qu'il faisait?
   a. Il faisait des obstructions sur ce qu'il voyait.
   b. Il faisait des obsessions sur ce qu'il voyait.
   c. Il faisait des observations sur ce qu'il voyait.

6. Qu'est-ce que c'est qu'un salon?
   a. C'est un endroit où se réunissaient les trompés, les trompeurs et les trompettes.
   b. C'est un endroit où se réunissaient les touristes, les trompeurs et les trompettes.
   c. C'est un endroit où se réunissaient les trompés, les trompeurs et les cacahuètes.

7. Un trompé...
   a. joue de la trompette.
   b. est quelqu'un qu'on a trompé.
   c. circule des rumeurs.

8. Un trompeur...
   a. trompe les gens.
   b. trompe les troupeaux.
   c. triche aux cartes.

This is the end of the taped activities for Chapter 14.

A. Scénario. Listen to the surprise that occurs when the students set out to see the monuments of Paris. You may not understand every word, but you should be able to follow the story line.

NARRATOR: Le lendemain matin, les quatre amis décident de voir quelques monuments à Paris. Ils essaient de se décider sur le meilleur itinéraire. Ils s'asseyent à la terrasse d'un café. Le garçon arrive et prend leurs commandes. Tout d'un coup, ils voient un jeune homme attaquer un monsieur. Les quatre sautent de leur chaise et se précipitent vers le pauvre homme. Le jeune pickpocket s'enfuit et le monsieur tombe par terre.

LE MONSIEUR: Mais qu'est-ce qui s'est passé? Qui êtes-vous?

HENRY: Quelqu'un vous a agressé pour voler votre portefeuille. Et moi, je suis un étudiant américain...

LE MONSIEUR: Mais avec qui êtes-vous?

HENRY: Je suis là avec mes amis.

LE MONSIEUR: Lequel a vu cet incident?

TOUS LES QUATRE AMIS: Nous l'avons tous vu.

LE MONSIEUR: Je vous demande pardon. J'ai été brusque avec vous.

MARGUERITE: Nous comprenons bien, monsieur. Après tout, vous avez reçu un coup.

NARRATOR: La police arrive.

L'AGENT DE POLICE: Monsieur, comment vous sentez-vous? Voulez-vous que j'appelle le S.A.M.U.?

NARRATOR: Le vieux monsieur hoche la tête.

L'AGENT DE POLICE: Alors, quel âge le pickpocket pouvait-il avoir? De quelle couleur étaient ses cheveux? Ses yeux?

NARRATOR: L'agent de police trouve un ticket de train par terre. Il le ramasse.

L'AGENT DE POLICE: Mais, qu'est-ce que c'est?

HENRY: Mais, ce n'est pas possible. Quelle coïncidence! C'est le gentil monsieur que nous avons rencontré dans le train.

B. A vous maintenant! Listen again to the **scénario** and repeat during the pauses. Pay particular attention to pronunciation and intonation.

NARRATOR: Le lendemain matin,//les quatre amis décident de voir // quelques monuments à Paris.// Ils essaient de se décider // sur le meilleur itinéraire.// Ils s'asseyent à la terrasse d'un café.// Le garçon arrive // et prend leurs commandes.// Tout d'un coup,// ils voient un jeune homme attaquer // un monsieur.// Les quatre sautent de leur chaise // et se précipitent vers le pauvre homme.// Le jeune pickpocket s'enfuit // et le monsieur tombe par terre.//

LE MONSIEUR: Mais qu'est-ce qui s'est passé?// Qui êtes-vous?//

HENRY: Quelqu'un vous a agressé // pour voler votre portefeuille.// Et moi,// je suis un étudiant américain... //

LE MONSIEUR: Mais avec qui êtes-vous?//

HENRY: Je suis là // avec mes amis.//

LE MONSIEUR: Lequel a vu cet incident?//

TOUS LES QUATRE AMIS: Nous l'avons tous vu.//

LE MONSIEUR: Je vous demande pardon.// J'ai été brusque avec vous.//

MARGUERITE: Nous comprenons bien, monsieur.// Après tout,// vous avez reçu un coup.//

NARRATOR: La police arrive.//

L'AGENT DE POLICE: Monsieur, comment vous sentez-vous?// Voulez-vous que j'appelle // le S.A.M.U.?//

NARRATOR: Le vieux monsieur hoche la tête.//

L'AGENT DE POLICE: Alors, quel âge le pickpocket // pouvait-il avoir?// De quelle couleur // étaient ses cheveux?// Ses yeux?//

NARRATOR: L'agent de police trouve // un ticket de train par terre.// Il le ramasse.//

L'AGENT DE POLICE: Mais, qu'est-ce que c'est?//

HENRY: Mais, ce n'est pas possible.// Quelle coïncidence!// C'est le gentil monsieur // que nous avons rencontré dans le train.//

C. La journée de Jean-Paul. Jean-Paul is telling what he did today, but he isn't being very specific. What would you say to get more information? Listen to each of Jean-Paul's statements. Then select the form of **lequel** you would use to respond. Circle the letter of the appropriate response.

1. Ce matin j'ai visité la cathédrale.
2. J'ai regardé les beaux vitraux.
3. A midi, j'ai téléphoné à un ami.
4. Mon ami et moi, nous avons déjeuné au café.
5. Nous avons parlé de son prof.
6. Après le déjeuner, nous sommes allés au musée.
7. J'ai beaucoup apprécié le chef-d'œuvre magnifique.
8. Malheureusement, au musée j'ai perdu mes billets.

D. La cuisine des Martin. Monsieur Martin is cleaning the kitchen and taking an inventory of things. Listen as he tells Madame Martin how many of each kitchen item they have. Then circle the letter of the expression that best corresponds to the number he has given.

1. Ah... nous avons trente-huit couteaux.
2. Il y a cinquante-sept serviettes.
3. Voici treize casseroles.
4. Il y a dix-neuf tasses.
5. Nous avons trente-deux assiettes.
6. Il y a neuf nappes.

E. Non, non, non! Alice is asking her cousin Thomas lots of questions. Because Thomas thinks Alice is a pest, he isn't being very polite with her and answers every question negatively. Listen to each of Alice's questions and circle the letter of the more logical response.

1. Tu as vu le film de Gérard Depardieu à la télé hier soir?
   a. Non, je n'ai vu personne.
   b. Non, je ne regarde jamais la télé.

2. Tu détestes les légumes, n'est-ce pas?
   a. Oui, ce soir je n'ai mangé aucun légume.
   b. Oui, ce soir je n'ai mangé que des légumes et du poulet.

3. Tu aimes les pommes et les poires, n'est-ce pas?
   a. C'est vrai. Je n'aime ni pommes ni poires.
   b. Non, je n'aime pas les fruits.

4. Qui t'a donné ton portefeuille?
   a. Rien.
   b. Personne.

5. Tu peux me prêter vingt francs?
   a. Non, je n'ai que cent francs.
   b. Non, je n'ai plus d'argent.

F. Allons encore plus loin. You will hear a passage that expands on this chapter's vocabulary and grammar. Listen carefully as the passage is read twice. You may not understand every word, but you should be able to follow the story line. You will then hear a series of questions and possible answers. Based on your understanding of the story, circle the letter of the best answer to each question.

Eugène Ionesco

Eugène Ionesco a écrit *Rhinocéros*, pièce de théâtre où il condamne le conformisme. Un beau dimanche matin, deux amis, Jean et Bérenger, sont assis à la terrasse d'un café. Peu après, un rhinocéros court dans la rue. C'est le premier d'une grande série de rhinocéros qui apparaîtront plus tard. Tous les amis de Bérenger, les uns après les autres, deviennent rhinocéros, c'est-à-dire tous les gens du village succombent à l'idée de devenir rhinocéros, de se ressembler en toute chose et de se soumettre à l'esprit de la foule. A la fin, une seule personne refuse de capituler: Bérenger, le héros de l'histoire. Et, lui, ne sait pas exactement pourquoi il y résiste, mais il ne peut pas supporter l'idée de devenir comme les autres.

1. Qu'est-ce que c'est que *Rhinocéros*?
   a. Un animal qu'on trouve en Afrique.
   b. Un animal qui est énorme.
   c. Le nom d'une pièce de Ionesco.

2. Qu'est-ce que l'auteur condamne dans la pièce?
   a. Il condamne le compliment.
   b. Il condamne le conformisme.
   c. Il condamne la contemplation.

3. Qu'est-ce qui se passe un dimanche matin?
   a. Deux amis sont endormis à la terrasse d'un café.
   b. Deux amis sont assis à la terrasse d'un café.
   c. Deux amis sont assez.

4. Qu'est-ce qui se passe peu après?
   a. Un rhinocéros court dans la rue.
   b. Un rhinocéros bouge dans la rue.
   c. Un rhinocéros boude dans la rue.

5. Qui devient rhinocéros?
   a. Bérenger.
   b. Tous les gens, sauf Bérenger.
   c. Eugène Ionesco.

6. Pourquoi Bérenger résiste-t-il à l'idée de devenir rhinocéros?
   a. Parce qu'il peut supporter l'idée de devenir comme les autres.
   b. Parce qu'il voudrait devenir rhinocéros.
   c. Parce qu'il ne peut pas supporter l'idée de devenir comme les autres.

This is the end of the taped activities for Chapter 15.

A. Scénario. Listen as Robert, Nicole, and Monsieur Fourchet discuss careers. You may not understand every word, but you should be able to follow the story line.

M. FOURCHET: Quel est le métier de ton père, Robert?
ROBERT: Mon père est avocat à New York.
M. FOURCHET: Et ta mère, travaille-t-elle?
ROBERT: Elle est chirurgienne.
M. FOURCHET: Ce qui m'intéresse est de savoir ce que vous voulez devenir.
ROBERT: J'espère devenir médecin, comme Nicole.
NICOLE: Moi? Jamais de la vie! Tu te trompes. Je ne veux devenir ni médecin, ni infirmière.
ROBERT: Ne te fâche pas! C'était juste pour plaisanter.
M. FOURCHET: Sérieusement, quel métier choisiras-tu quand tu finiras tes études?
ROBERT: Si j'étais meilleur en biologie, je deviendrais chirurgien, comme ma mère.
NICOLE: J'aimerais beaucoup devenir architecte.
M. FOURCHET: Mais il faudra que tu te spécialises!
NICOLE: Oui, je le sais. L'amie dont je t'ai parlé a fait la même chose.

B. A vous maintenant! Listen again to the **scénario** and repeat during the pauses. Pay particular attention to pronunciation and intonation.

M. FOURCHET: Quel est le métier de ton père,// Robert?//
ROBERT: Mon père est avocat // à New York.//
M. FOURCHET: Et ta mère,// travaille-t-elle?//
ROBERT: Elle est chirurgienne.//
M. FOURCHET: Ce qui m'intéresse // est de savoir // ce que vous voulez devenir.//
ROBERT: J'espère devenir médecin,// comme Nicole.//
NICOLE: Moi? Jamais de la vie!// Tu te trompes.// Je ne veux devenir // ni médecin, ni infirmière.//
ROBERT: Ne te fâche pas!// C'était juste pour plaisanter.//
M. FOURCHET: Sérieusement,// quel métier choisiras-tu // quand tu finiras tes études?//
ROBERT: Si j'étais meilleur en biologie,// je deviendrais chirurgien,// comme ma mère.//
NICOLE: J'aimerais beaucoup // devenir architecte.//
M. FOURCHET: Mais il faudra // que tu te spécialises!//
NICOLE: Oui, je le sais.// L'amie dont je t'ai parlé // a fait la même chose.//

C. Spécialisations. You will hear nine statements describing different students' interests and fields of study. Write the number of each statement under the appropriate picture.

1. Caroline veut devenir médecin. Alors, cette année à l'université, elle suit plusieurs cours de chimie.

2. Mon ami Alexandre s'intéresse aux beaux-arts. Il se spécialise en peinture.

3. Jean-Claude pense qu'il voudrait être interprète. Alors il se spécialise en langues modernes.

4. Ma sœur Nicole choisira le métier de notre père, qui est diplomate. Elle suit plusieurs cours de sciences politiques.

5. Marie-France, qui espère devenir informaticienne, suit trois cours d'informatique cette année.

6. Georges se spécialise en histoire parce qu'il veut un jour écrire des romans historiques.

7. Robert aime bien les maths et il espère devenir comptable.

8. Henry croit qu'il veut devenir professeur de philosophie. Il suit deux cours de philosophie cette année.

9. Jeanne se spécialise en psychologie; elle veut devenir psychologue.

D. Les études de Dominique. Dominique's friends are speculating about his studies and work habits. Some of the statements tell what the speakers think Dominique *will do,* and some tell what Dominique *would do* under certain conditions. Indicate whether each statement tells what Dominique will do **(futur)** or what he would do **(conditionnel).**

1. Je pense que Dominique étudiera les sciences politiques l'année prochaine.
2. S'il était plus doué en sciences, il pourrait devenir médecin.
3. Si tu l'aidais, il réussirait au prochain examen de maths.
4. S'il ne va pas à la plage ce week-end, il finira les devoirs d'histoire.
5. Dominique dit qu'il ira à la conférence samedi matin.
6. Dominique aimerait bien réussir à tous ses examens cette année.
7. Le père de Dominique espère qu'il deviendra homme d'affaires.
8. Que fera Dominique?

E. Madame Martin. Madame Martin is very proud of her grandchildren. Listen as she tells what each of them does for a living and write the number of each description under the appropriate picture.

1. Ma petite-fille Nicole travaille comme banquière à Paris.
2. Mon petit-fils David travaille comme cuisinier dans un restaurant formidable!
3. Danièle est si artistique! Elle est architecte à Rome.
4. Claude est très intelligent. Il travaille comme informaticien à Bordeaux.
5. Ma petite Michèle est facteur à Avignon.
6. Alexandre est très gentil. Il est agent de police à Paris.

F. Allons encore plus loin. You will hear a passage that expands on this chapter's vocabulary and grammar. Listen carefully as the passage is read twice. You may not understand every word, but you should be able to follow the story line. You will then hear a series of questions and possible answers. Based on your understanding of the story, circle the letter of the best answer to each question.

Maurice Maeterlinck

Maurice Maeterlinck est né en Belgique en 1862 et est mort en 1949. Il a écrit des essais et des pièces de théâtre en français qui lui ont fait gagner le Prix Nobel en 1911. Un de ses chefs-d'œuvre est *Pelléas et Mélisande*, un drame profondément symboliste dont Debussy a fait un opéra. Maeterlinck croyait qu'il y avait deux mondes: un monde visible, celui que nous occupons, et un monde invisible, celui qu'habitent des forces occultes. Le monde invisible essaie toujours de communiquer avec le monde visible pour nous prévenir de toutes sortes de dangers. Le symbole est le moyen de communication qu'emploie le monde invisible. Malheureusement, nous ne sommes pas toujours capables d'interpréter ces symboles parce que la simplicité nous manque. Les enfants, par contre, parviennent à découvrir naturellement le sens du symbole, mais ils ne sont pas toujours capables d'expliquer leur signification.

1. Où Maeterlinck est-il né?
   a. En Bretagne.
   b. Au Brésil.
   c. En Belgique.

2. Qu'est-ce qu'il a écrit?
   a. Des essais et des pièces de théâtre.
   b. Des essais et des pièces de thèses.
   c. Des essaims et des pièces de théâtre.

3. Qu'est-ce qu'il a gagné en 1911?
   a. Le Prix de noblesse.
   b. Le Prix Nobel.
   c. Le Prix Noble.

4. Quelle sorte de pièce est *Pelléas et Mélisande*?
   a. C'est une pièce symboliste.
   b. C'est une pièce sympathique.
   c. C'est une pièce simpliste.

5. Qu'est-ce que Debussy a fait de cette pièce?
   a. Un opérateur.
   b. Un opéra.
   c. Une optique.

6. Que fait le monde invisible?
   a. Il essaie de communiquer avec le monde visible.

b. Il essaie de communiquer visiblement.
c. Il essaie de communiquer avec les communistes.

7. Pourquoi le monde invisible essaie-t-il de communiquer?
   a. Pour envoyer un télégramme à ses amis.
   b. Pour nous prévenir de toutes sortes de dangers.
   c. Pour nous prévenir de toutes sortes de danses.

8. Pourquoi ne sommes-nous pas capables d'interpréter les messages du monde invisible?
   a. Parce que nous sommes trop simples.
   b. Parce que nous ne sommes pas sérieux.
   c. Parce que nous ne sommes pas suffisamment simples.

9. Les enfants, que font-ils?
   a. Les enfants parviennent à découvrir le centre de la ville.
   b. Les enfants parviennent à découvrir le sens du symbole.
   c. Les enfants parviennent à découvrir la porte de la maison.

10. Quel problème les enfants ont-ils?
    a. Ils sont trop jeunes pour apprendre le français.
    b. Ils sont très timides pour expliquer leurs leçons.
    c. Ils ne peuvent pas expliquer la signification des messages.

This is the end of the taped activities for Chapter 16.

A. Scénario. Listen to the conversations as Henry and his friends gather at a café. You may not understand every word, but you should be able to follow the story line.

ROBERT: Aïe! Je me suis coupé. Il faut que je rentre chez moi. J'essaierai de te retrouver au café. Il est possible que je sois un peu en retard. Sinon, je te téléphonerai.
PIERRE: D'accord!
NARRATOR: David sort du gymnase.
DAVID: Pourquoi part-il comme une flèche?
PIERRE: Il retourne chez lui pour se mettre un pansement. Allons au café!
NARRATOR: Ils rencontrent Alain en route et l'invitent à les accompagner. Alain se présente à Henry et à Sylvie qui sont toujours au café.
PIERRE: Ah, bon! Vous voilà. Vous vous souvenez, pendant le match, quand...
SYLVIE: Ecoutez, j'en ai ras le bol d'entendre parler sports tout le temps. Vos histoires manquent d'intérêt. N'y a-t-il rien d'autre qui compte pour vous? N'avez-vous pas un violon d'Ingres, par exemple?
HENRY: Oh, si! Tu tombes bien! Tous les membres de l'équipe jouent d'un instrument de musique. Nous pourrions aussi bien former un orchestre.
SYLVIE: Ça vaudrait mieux et ça nous casserait moins les oreilles.

B. A vous maintenant! Listen again to the **scénario** and repeat during the pauses. Pay particular attention to the pronunciation and intonation.

ROBERT: Aïe!// Je me suis coupé.// Il faut que je rentre chez moi.// J'essaierai de te retrouver au café.// Il est possible // que je sois un peu en retard.// Sinon, je te téléphonerai.//
PIERRE: D'accord!//
NARRATOR: David sort du gymnase.//
DAVID: Pourquoi part-il // comme une flèche?//
PIERRE: Il retourne chez lui // pour se mettre // un pansement.// Allons au café!//
NARRATOR: Ils rencontrent Alain en route // et l'invitent à les accompagner.// Alain se présente à Henry // et à Sylvie // qui sont toujours au café.//
PIERRE: Ah, bon! Vous voilà.// Vous vous souvenez,// pendant le match, quand... //
SYLVIE: Ecoutez, j'en ai ras le bol // d'entendre parler sports tout le temps.// Vos histoires manquent d'intérêt.// N'y a-t-il rien d'autre qui compte pour vous?// N'avez-vous pas // un violon d'Ingres,// par exemple?//
HENRY: Oh, si!// Tu tombes bien!// Tous les membres de l'équipe jouent // d'un instrument de musique.// Nous pourrions aussi bien // former un orchestre.//
SYLVIE: Ça vaudrait mieux // et ça nous casserait moins // les oreilles.//

C. Des jeux. Several students are discussing what to do during a break from classes. Write the number of each statement under the picture that corresponds to what the person wants to do.

1. Je voudrais aller au parc jouer au tennis.
2. Moi, je voudrais passer l'après-midi dans le gymnase. Tu sais que j'adore le basket-ball.
3. Moi, je suis fatiguée et je voudrais me reposer un peu. Allons au café pour jouer aux cartes.
4. Caroline et moi, nous allons jouer au golf cet après-midi. Qui veut nous accompagner?
5. Si nous jouions au football?
6. Moi, je veux regarder un match de base-ball à la télé.

D. Des musiciens. Let's test your knowledge of famous musicians. Listen to the following clues and write the number of each sentence under the picture of the instrument it best describes.

1. Liberace qui portait des vêtements brillants jouait de cet instrument.
2. Quand Ringo Starr était avec les Beatles, il jouait de cet instrument.
3. Dexter Gordon qui a vécu longtemps à Paris et qui a joué dans le film «Round Midnight» jouait de cet instrument.
4. Louis Amstrong, appelé aussi Sachmo, jouait de cet instrument.
5. Benny Goodman et Woody Allen préfèrent cet instrument.
6. Itzhak Perlman joue de cet instrument dont les meilleurs sont des Stradivarius.
7. Carlos Santana est très connu pour jouer de cet instrument.

E. Le week-end. Monsieur and Madame Etienne are going away for a long weekend and are sending their teenage children, Marianne and Pierre, to spend the time with their grandparents. When the Etiennes give the children instructions, the children respond that of course they will do everything they are told to do. Listen to each statement by Monsieur and Madame Etienne. Then complete the corresponding response of the children, using a phrase that includes an infinitive.

Modèle: — Il faut que vous mangiez beaucoup de légumes.
— *Oui, il faut manger beaucoup de légumes.*

1. Marianne et Pierre, il faut que vous alliez chez vos grands-parents ce week-end.
2. Nous préférons que vous ne conduisiez pas la voiture.
3. Il est nécessaire que vous preniez l'autobus pour y aller.
4. Pierre, pendant le week-end il faut que tu fasses tes devoirs.
5. Marianne, je veux que tu lises ce roman.
6. Marianne, je doute que tu puisses jouer au golf.

7. Mais nous sommes heureux que vous jouiez aux cartes avec grand-papa.
8. Et il est nécessaire que vous dormiez assez.
9. Et n'oubliez pas! Il faut que vous soyez toujours polis.

F. Allons encore plus loin. You will hear a passage that expands on this chapter's vocabulary and grammar. Listen carefully as the passage is read twice. You may not understand every word, but you should be able to follow the story line. You will then hear a series of questions and possible answers. Based on your understanding of the story, circle the letter of the best answer to each question.

Sarah Bernhart

Sarah Bernhart est née à Paris en 1844 et y est morte en 1923. Sa vie elle-même a été un drame extraordinaire. Pendant sa carrière théâtrale, elle a joué les plus grands rôles avec une maîtrise qu'on n'a jamais égalée. Elle avait une mémoire prodigieuse, un talent remarquable en tant que peintre-artiste, sculpteur, écrivain et professeur. Elle était douée d'un vaste sens de l'humain et on a loué son héroïsme et son appui pour Dreyfus. L'écrivain Marcel Proust parle d'elle dans son roman *A la recherche du temps perdu*, où il la décrit comme Berma dans le rôle de Phèdre. On a dû lui couper la jambe droite en 1918. Beaucoup la considère comme la tragédienne la plus brillante de l'époque moderne.

1. En quelle année et où Sarah Bernhart est-elle née?
   a. Elle est née en 1844 à Bruxelles.
   b. Elle est née en 1844 à Brooklyn.
   c. Elle est née en 1844 à Paris.

2. Quelle a été sa vie?
   a. Un drame extraordinaire.
   b. Un drame ordinaire.
   c. Un drame moderne.

3. Qu'est-ce qu'elle avait?
   a. Une mémoire prodigieuse.
   b. Une mémoire prolifique.
   c. Une mémoire professionnelle.

4. Ses autres caractéristiques lui permettaient...
   a. de peindre, de sculpter, d'écrire, d'enseigner.
   b. de peindre, de sculpter, d'écrire, de renseigner.
   c. de peindre, de sculpter, de crier, d'enseigner.

5. De quoi était-elle douée?
   a. D'un vaste sens de l'humour.
   b. D'un vaste sens de l'humain.
   c. D'un vaste sens de l'amour.

6. Qui parle d'elle dans un roman?
   a. Marcel Broust.
   b. Marcel Caillou.
   c. Marcel Proust.

7. Dans quel rôle la décrit-il?
   a. Dans le rôle de Berma.
   b. Dans le rôle de Thelma.
   c. Dans le rôle de Phèdre.

8. Qu'est-ce qu'on a dû lui couper?
   a. Sa jambe gauche.
   b. Son bras droit.
   c. Sa jambe droite.

9. Comment la considère-t-on?
   a. L'actrice la plus compliquée de l'époque moderne.
   b. L'actrice la plus brillante de l'époque moderne.
   c. L'actrice la plus riche de l'époque moderne.

This is the end of the taped activities for Chapter 17.

A. Scénario. Listen to the conversation as the students discuss what kinds of movies they like. You may not understand every word, but you should be able to follow the story line.

NARRATOR: Au lux, on passe un film policier.
HENRY: J'aime ce genre de films. J'adore le suspense.
PIERRE: Moi, pas! Ils sont comme tous les films américains et je n'en aime aucun.
SYLVIE: On réfléchit avant d'ouvrir la bouche. Donne-nous au moins une bonne raison!
PIERRE: Il y a trop de violence, il n'y a pas assez de psychologie et, si les acteurs sont beaux, ils ne savent pas jouer.
FRANCINE: C'est plutôt idiot, ce que tu racontes là, non? Nos films ne sont guère différents.
HENRY: Ça va, ça va. Ne vous emballez pas! Allons-y! Je ne crois pas qu'il soit si difficile de se mettre d'accord. Nous discuterons après.
NARRATOR: Après la séance...
HENRY: Alors, tu as changé d'avis maintenant que tu as vu le film?
PIERRE: Absolument pas!
SYLVIE: J'ai peur que tu n'exagères. Tu me fais rire.
MARGUERITE: Il faut que tu comprennes le but du film.
PIERRE: Il semble que le metteur en scène n'en ait pas eu.
SYLVIE: Moi, j'ai aimé le film. Le jeu était bien mené et les acteurs étaient tout à fait dans la peau de leurs personnages.
MARGUERITE: Chacun à son goût.

B. A vous maintenant! Listen again to the **scénario** and repeat during the pauses. Pay particular attention to pronunciation and intonation.

NARRATOR: Au Lux, on passe un film policier.//
HENRY: J'aime ce genre de films.// J'adore le suspense.//
PIERRE: Moi, pas!// Ils sont comme tous les films américains // et je n'en aime aucun.//
SYLVIE: On réfléchit // avant d'ouvrir la bouche.// Donne-nous au moins // une bonne raison!//
PIERRE: Il y a trop de violence,// il n'y a pas assez de psychologie // et, si les acteurs sont beaux,// ils ne savent pas jouer.//
FRANCINE: C'est plutôt idiot,// ce que tu racontes là, non?// Nos films ne sont guère différents.//
HENRY: Ça va, ça va.// Ne vous emballez pas!// Allons-y!// Je ne crois pas // qu'il soit si difficile // de se mettre d'accord.// Nous discuterons après.//
NARRATOR: Après la séance... //
HENRY: Alors, tu as changé d'avis // maintenant que tu as vu le film?//

PIERRE: Absolument pas!//
SYLVIE: J'ai peur que tu n'exagères.// Tu me fais rire.//
MARGUERITE: Il faut que tu comprennes // le but du film.//
PIERRE: Il semble que // le metteur en scène n'en ait pas eu.//
SYLVIE: Moi, j'ai aimé le film.// Le jeu était bien mené // et les acteurs étaient // tout à fait dans la peau de leurs personnages.//
MARGUERITE: Chacun à son goût.//

C. On peut voir... A group of friends is discussing what to do this weekend. Write the number of each suggestion under the appropriate picture.

1. Au Rex on passe un film américain doublé. Vous voulez le voir?
2. Je voudrais aller au théâtre. On peut y voir une tragi-comédie excellente.
3. Moi, je préfère voir la revue musicale au Forum.
4. Allons au Palace où on passe un western américain en version originale.
5. Non, allons à l'université où on passe un bon documentaire canadien.
6. Tu connais la sœur de Daniel? Elle est chanteuse célèbre. Allons la voir à l'opérette.
7. Moi, je préfère la danse. Allons au ballet.

D. Pauvre Jean-Claude. Jean-Claude overslept this morning and was in a hurry to get to work. Listen to the description of his morning and complete each sentence based on what you hear.

1. Jean-Claude a dormi trop tard ce matin. Etant pressé, il n'a pas pris de petit déjeuner.
2. Il a bu du café en se rasant.
3. Il a jeté un coup d'œil sur le journal en s'habillant.
4. Ayant beaucoup à faire, il voulait partir de bonne heure.
5. Prenant son manteau, il est sorti de la maison.
6. Malheureusement, en sortant de la maison, il est tombé.
7. Pauvre Jean-Claude! En conduisant au bureau, il a reçu une contravention.

E. Allons encore plus loin. You will hear a passage that expands on this chapter's vocabulary and grammar. Listen carefully as the passage is read twice. You may not understand every word, but you should be able to follow the story line. You will then hear a series of questions and possible answers. Based on your understanding of the story, circle the letter of the best answer to each question.

James Bond

James Bond est un agent secret au service de la reine d'Angleterre. Il a été entraîné par les meilleurs experts dans toutes les catégories d'arts martiaux, comme le judo et le karaté. On lui a appris à maîtriser les armes à feu et à être un bon espion. Il a aussi appris à piloter toutes sortes d'avions, de voitures et de bateaux. Après s'être distingué dans chacune de ces disciplines, on lui a accordé le titre 007, ce qui lui a donné des droits spéciaux, dont celui de tuer. James Bond est aussi un grand gourmet et un fin connaisseur de vins.

1. Quel est le métier de James Bond?
   a. Agent de police.
   b. Agent de presse.
   c. Agent secret.

2. Au service de qui est-il?
   a. La reine d'Angola.
   b. La reine d'Angleterre.
   c. La reine d'Allemagne.

3. Par qui a-t-il été entraîné?
   a. Par les meilleurs préfets.
   b. Par les meilleurs experts.
   c. Par les meilleurs suspects.

4. Dans quelles catégories d'arts martiaux a-t-il été entraîné?
   a. Le yoga et le karaté.
   b. Le judo et le karaté.
   c. Le judo et les qualités.

5. Qu'est-ce qu'il a appris à piloter?
   a. Des avions, des voitures, des bestiaux.
   b. Des avions, des voisins, des bateaux.
   c. Des avions, des voitures, des bateaux.

6. Quel titre lui a-t-on accordé?
   a. 017.
   b. 707.
   c. 007.

7. Qu'est-ce qu'on lui a accordé de plus?
   a. Des droits spécieux.
   b. Des droits spéciaux.
   c. Des droits sceptiques.

8. James Bond a aussi la réputation d'être...
   a. un gros gourmet.
   b. un grand gourmand.
   c. un grand gourmet.

9. Et il est aussi un fin...
   a. connaisseur de vent.
   b. connaisseur de vins.
   c. connaisseur de vingt.

This is the end of the taped activities for Chapter 18.

A. Scénario. Listen as the students visit a French village and meet the mayor. You may not understand every word, but you should be able to follow the story line.

NARRATOR: A la fin des cours, le professeur avait proposé aux étudiants une expérience culturelle. Les étudiants iraient visiter un village et rédigeraient un rapport. En tirant au sort le nom d'un village, Robert, Henry et Marguerite sont tombés sur le village de Valençay. Les trois amis auraient pris le train s'ils avaient eu assez d'argent, mais ils s'y sont rendus en faisant de l'auto-stop. Les voici au village de Valençay.

HENRY: Par quoi commence-t-on? As-tu une idée?

ROBERT: Si on commençait par cet épicier? Il connaît beaucoup de monde.

MARGUERITE: Le village a environ trois mille habitants. C'est sûrement le maire qui connaît le mieux les gens et sait ce qui se passe dans son village. Essayons d'avoir un tête-à-tête avec lui.

ROBERT: D'accord, mais passons d'abord par le bureau de poste. J'ai besoin de timbres avant de mettre mes cartes postales à la boîte.

NARRATOR: Un peu plus tard, chez le maire...

MARGUERITE: Monsieur le Maire, notre professeur nous a demandé de visiter votre village et de rassembler autant d'informations que possible pour en faire un compte-rendu.

ROBERT: Nous aimerions bien vous poser quelques questions.

LE MAIRE: Puisque c'est l'heure du repas, je vous invite à le partager avec nous à la bonne franquette. Ma femme sera heureuse de faire votre connaissance.

B. A vous maintenant! Listen again to the **scénario** and repeat during the pauses. Pay particular attention to pronunciation and intonation.

NARRATOR: A la fin des cours,// le professeur avait proposé aux étudiants // une expérience culturelle.// Les étudiants iraient visiter un village // et rédigeraient un rapport.// En tirant au sort le nom d'un village,// Robert, Henry et Marguerite sont tombés // sur le village de Valençay.// Les trois amis auraient pris le train // s'ils avaient eu assez d'argent,// mais ils s'y sont rendus // en faisant de l'auto-stop.// Les voici au village de Valençay.//

HENRY: Par quoi commence-t-on?// As-tu une idée?//

ROBERT: Si on commençait par cet épicier?// Il connaît beaucoup de monde.//

MARGUERITE: Le village a // environ trois mille habitants.// C'est sûrement // le maire qui connaît // le mieux les gens // et sait ce qui se passe // dans son village.// Essayons d'avoir // un tête-à-tête avec lui.//

ROBERT: D'accord,// mais passons d'abord // par le bureau de poste.// J'ai besoin de timbres // avant de mettre // mes cartes postales à la boîte.//

NARRATOR: Un peu plus tard,// chez le maire... //

MARGUERITE: Monsieur le Maire,// notre professeur nous a demandé // de visiter votre village // et de rassembler autant d'informations que possible // pour en faire un compte-rendu.//

ROBERT: Nous aimerions bien // vous poser quelques questions.//

LE MAIRE: Puisque c'est l'heure du repas,// je vous invite à le partager // avec nous à la bonne franquette.// Ma femme sera heureuse // de faire votre connaissance.//

C. A choisir! Circle the verb whose meaning best fits each of the five descriptions you hear. Follow the model.

couvrir ouvrir découvrir souffrir offrir

Modèle: On fait ça avec un bouquet de fleurs.
offrir

1. On fait ça avec la porte.
2. On fait ça quand on est très triste ou très malade.
3. On fait ça avec quelque chose de nouveau.
4. On fait ça au lit avec des draps et une couverture.
5. On fait ça quand on donne un cadeau.

D. Le plus-que-parfait. Listen to the following sentences describing different scenes. Notice that in each case, one action was finished before the next one took place. Circle the verb that represents the action that took place first.

1. J'avais fait le ménage quand vous êtes arrivé.
2. Nous avions fini de dîner quand il est revenu.
3. Ils avaient dansé quand les autres sont venus.
4. Ils s'étaient assis à table quand le téléphone a sonné.
5. Il était parti quand je suis arrivé.
6. Il a voulu commencer quand les autres avaient fini de jouer.

E. Les regrets. You will hear several people tell about things that just weren't quite right today. Listen to each statement, decide what the person should have done, and complete the response using one of the phrases from the list. Follow the model.

Modèle: Paul n'avait pas beaucoup d'énergie.
Il aurait dû faire la sieste.

1. En essayant de téléphoner à ma cousine, j'ai composé le mauvais numéro.
2. Annie a laissé la porte ouverte toute la nuit!

3. Les Dupont sont allés à l'aéroport ce matin, mais l'avion était complet.
4. Nous sortions ce matin quand le téléphone a sonné et nous n'y avons pas répondu. Je pense que c'était important.
5. Tu avais mal à la tête?
6. Je voulais envoyer une lettre, mais je n'avais pas de timbres.

F. Allons encore plus loin. You will hear a passage that expands on this chapter's vocabulary and grammar. Listen carefully as the passage is read twice. You may not understand every word, but you should be able to follow the story line. You will then hear a series of questions and possible answers. Based on your understanding of the story, circle the letter of the best answer to each question.

Van Gogh à Arles

Vincent Van Gogh est né en Hollande en 1853. D'abord, il est allé à Paris en février 1886, puis s'est installé à Arles en 1888 dans un état déplorable. Il voulait y créer un atelier où des artistes vivraient en commun. Paul Gaughin devint le premier et le seul membre de cette société. Van Gogh était très humble à l'égard de ce que nous considérons ses plus admirables chefs-d'œuvre. C'est à Arles et dans ses environs qu'il a peint plusieurs tableaux — entre autres, *les Iris*, *les Tournesols*, *le Pont de Trinquetaille* [ou *le Pont de l'Anglais à Arles*], *la Nuit étoilée*, *le Champ de blé aux corbeaux* [ou *les Blés jaunes]*. Ses tableaux reflètent son esprit troublé et le feu intérieur qui l'a poussé à créer son œuvre. Il a passé quatorze mois à Arles d'où il écrit beaucoup de lettres à son frère Théo pour lui demander de l'aide monétaire. En raison de troubles psychologiques, Van Gogh a été interné un an à l'asile Saint-Paul à Saint-Rémy. Après une dernière visite à Paris chez son frère, qu'il a trouvé préoccupé par une situation difficile, il s'est suicidé et est mort le 27 juillet 1890.

1. Où et quand est né Van Gogh?
   a. En Hollande, en 1853.
   b. En France, en 1853.
   c. En Belgique, en 1853.

2. Où s'est-il installé en 1888?
   a. A Arles.
   b. En Alsace.
   c. A Paris.

3. Comment y est-il arrivé?
   a. Dans un autobus.
   b. Dans un état déplorable.
   c. Dans un état démonstratif.

4. Qui fut le premier et seul membre de l'atelier?
   a. Paul Gaughin.

b. Paul Bonaparte.
c. Paul Gaudin.

5. Quelle était l'attitude de Van Gogh à l'égard de son œuvre?
   a. Très modeste.
   b. Très humble.
   c. Très arrogante.

6. Que nous montrent ses tableaux?
   a. Son esprit troublé et un feu à l'intérieur de sa maison.
   b. Son esprit troublé et un feu intérieur.
   c. Son esprit troublé et le feu de son foie.

7. Qu'est-ce qu'il demandait à son frère?
   a. De l'aide monétaire.
   b. De l'aide numéraire.
   c. De l'aide astrologique.

8. Pourquoi Van Gogh a-t-il été interné à l'asile Saint-Paul-de-Mausole?
   a. En raison de troubles financiers.
   b. En raison de troubles psychologiques.
   c. En raison de troubles philosophiques.

9. Quand est-ce qu'il est mort?
   a. Le 29 juillet 1870
   b. Le 28 juillet 1880.
   c. Le 27 juillet 1890.

This is the end of the taped activities for Chapter 19.

A. Scénario. Listen to the conversations surrounding Robert's trip to the post office to send a telegram. You may not understand every word, but you should be able to follow the story line.

ROBERT: Je serais resté ici bien plus longtemps si j'avais pu, mais maintenant que le stage se termine, je dois envoyer un télégramme aux Etats-Unis.
MME FOURCHET: Pourquoi pas téléphoner?
ROBERT: Parce que je connais ma mère, elle va me filer une liste de courses à faire dans les boutiques de Charles de Gaulle et je n'ai pas envie de faire cette corvée. Je veux seulement prévenir mes parents de mon heure d'arrivée.
MME FOURCHET: Téléphone tout de même! Ça leur fera plaisir de t'entendre. Ne te gêne pas pour te servir de notre téléphone! Vas-y!
ROBERT: Non, merci, je préfère envoyer un télégramme. J'irai au bureau de poste. Après tout, ce sera pour moi une expérience de plus.
NARRATOR: A la poste, il rencontre Nicole et Henry. Henry est en train d'acheter les derniers timbres sortis pour sa collection.
NICOLE: Tiens, salut! Que fais-tu ici?
ROBERT: Je vais envoyer un télégramme chez moi.
HENRY: Heureusement que tu m'y fais penser, il faut que j'envoie le mien aussi. Quand tu auras fini, j'enverrai le mien.
NARRATOR: Ils l'accompagnent au guichet.
L'EMPLOYE: ... dix-huit, dix-neuf... vous avez encore droit à trois mots pour le même prix.
ROBERT: «All my best.»
L'EMPLOYE: Qu'est-ce que cela veut dire?
ROBERT: C'est à peu près l'équivalent de: «Veuillez agréer, l'expression de mes sentiments les meilleurs».
L'EMPLOYE: Ça fait vingt-deux francs!
NARRATOR: Henry envoie aussi son télégramme et ils sortent de la poste en riant.
NICOLE: Sérieusement, mes amis, c'est dommage de vous voir partir. Vous avez fait des progrès sensass! Vous avez fait un bon job. C'est un bon show et tous les deux, vous êtes des stars. Vous êtes des super mecs!
HENRY ET ROBERT: Oh, là, là! Quel franglais!
NICOLE: Si, si, c'est vrai. Je dirai que vous parlez français vachement bien! Vous allez me manquer.
HENRY: Mais nous ne sommes pas encore partis... On va se revoir au dîner d'adieu.

B. A vous maintenant! Listen again to the **scénario** and repeat during the pauses. Pay particular attention to pronunciation and intonation.

ROBERT: Je serais resté ici // bien plus longtemps // si j'avais pu,// mais maintenant que le stage se termine,// je dois envoyer // un télégramme aux Etats-Unis.//

MME FOURCHET: Pourquoi pas téléphoner?//

ROBERT: Parce que je connais ma mère,// elle va me filer // une liste de courses à faire // dans les boutiques de Charles de Gaulle // et je n'ai pas envie // de faire cette corvée.// Je veux seulement // prévenir mes parents // de mon heure d'arrivée.//

MME FOURCHET: Téléphone tout de même!// Ça leur fera plaisir // de t'entendre.// Ne te gêne pas // pour te servir // de notre téléphone!// Vas-y!//

ROBERT: Non, merci, je préfère envoyer un télégramme.// J'irai au bureau de poste.// Après tout,// ce sera pour moi // une expérience de plus.//

NARRATOR: A la poste,// il rencontre Nicole et Henry.// Henry est en train d'acheter // les derniers timbres sortis // pour sa collection.//

NICOLE: Tiens, salut! // Que fais-tu ici?//

ROBERT: Je vais envoyer // un télégramme // chez moi.//

HENRY: Heureusement que tu m'y fais penser,// il faut que j'envoie // le mien aussi.// Quand tu auras fini,// j'enverrai le mien.//

NARRATOR: Ils l'accompagnent au guichet.//

L'EMPLOYE: ... dix-huit, dix-neuf... // vous avez encore droit à trois mots // pour le même prix.//

ROBERT: «All my best.»//

L'EMPLOYE: Qu'est-ce que cela veut dire?//

ROBERT: C'est à peu près // l'équivalent de:// «Veuillez agréer, l'expression de mes sentiments les meilleurs».//

L'EMPLOYE: Ça fait vingt-deux francs!//

NARRATOR: Henry envoie aussi son télégramme // et ils sortent de la poste en riant.//

NICOLE: Sérieusement, mes amis,// c'est dommage de vous voir partir.// Vous avez fait // des progrès sensass!// Vous avez fait un bon job.// C'est un bon show // et tous les deux,// vous êtes des stars.// Vous êtes des super mecs!//

HENRY ET ROBERT: Oh, là, là!// Quel franglais!//

NICOLE: Si, si, c'est vrai.// Je dirais que vous parlez français vachement bien! // Vous allez me manquer.//

HENRY: Mais nous ne sommes pas // encore partis... // On va se revoir // au dîner d'adieu.//

C. Au bureau de poste. Different people need to do certain things. Say which of the following things they'll need for each. Follow the model.

Modèle: Ma mère voudrait envoyer une lettre.// *Elle a besoin d'une boîte aux lettres et de timbres.*

1. Angélique voudrait envoyer un fax.// Elle a besoin d'un télécopieur.
2. David voudrait appeler Sylvie au numéro 55.61.72.99// Il a besoin d'un taxiphone.

3. Michèle et Anne voudraient envoyer un paquet.// Elles ont besoin de timbres.
4. Vous voudriez recevoir un fax.// Vous avez besoin d'un télécopieur.
5. Nous voudrions téléphoner à un ami. Nous n'avons pas le numéro.// Nous avons besoin d'un annuaire téléphonique et d'un taxiphone.

D. Scénario. Listen to the conversations that take place at the students' farewell party. You may not understand every word, but you should be able to follow the story line.

NARRATOR: Toutes les familles françaises sont réunies à l'Auberge du Vieux Moulin. Elles y sont avec leurs fils et leurs filles américains. Monsieur Galant, le propriétaire, a préparé un repas succulent. On entend la musique d'une chaîne stéréo. Il y a aussi un groupe de danseurs folkloriques qui, avec leur musique et leurs danses, régaleront la compagnie plus tard.

LE PROFESSEUR: ... et sans vous, nos pères et nos mères français, notre séjour aurait été simplement académique. Grâce à vous, nous avons habité dans vos foyers et partagé votre vie; vous nous avez accueillis chaleureusement. Si nous n'avions pas été hébergés par vous, nous n'aurions jamais connu la base de la culture française. Malgré la brièveté de notre séjour, nous nous sentons très proches des Français et emportons avec nous d'excellents souvenirs d'amitié qui ont créé des liens très forts entre nous.

ROBERT: Vous voyez, madame, c'est exactement ce que je ressens. Je cherchais mes mots pour vous dire la même chose.

MME FOURCHET: Nous gardons aussi un excellent souvenir de ton séjour. Combien de fromages as-tu goûtés chez nous? Tu t'en souviens?

ROBERT: Exactement soixante-six, ou un par jour.

MME FOURCHET: Alors, il faudra que tu reviennes pour goûter les deux cent soixante-quatorze qui restent! Et, en échange, tu nous feras goûter à la cuisine américaine. En attendant, mettons-nous à table et profitons de la bonne chère.

NARRATOR: Marguerite, Henry et Robert se retrouvent en aparté avant de passer à table.

HENRY: Ecoutez, chers amis, portons un toast à nos progrès en français! Nous avons tenu notre promesse, nous n'avons jamais parlé anglais ensemble et notre français est digne de...

MARGUERITE: ... digne de tous ceux qui le parlent dans le monde entier. A votre santé!

MARGUERITE, HENRY ET ROBERT: A la nôtre! A notre prochaine visite en France!

NARRATOR: A la fin de la soirée, tous se sont embrassés et on pouvait entendre la salle résonner de beaucoup de «au revoir» pleins de nostalgie et de promesses de s'écrire souvent.

E. A vous maintenant! Listen again to the **scénario** and repeat during the pauses. Pay particular attention to pronunciation and intonation.

NARRATOR: Toutes les familles françaises sont réunies // à l'Auberge du Vieux Moulin.// Elles y sont // avec leurs fils et leurs filles américains.// Monsieur Galant, le propriétaire,// a préparé un repas succulent.// On entend la musique // d'une chaîne stéréo.// Il y a aussi // un groupe de danseurs folkloriques qui,// avec leur musique et leurs danses,// régaleront la compagnie plus tard.//

LE PROFESSEUR: ... et sans vous,// nos pères et nos mères français,// notre séjour aurait été // simplement académique.// Grâce à vous,// nous avons habité dans vos foyers // et partagé votre vie;// vous nous avez accueillis chaleureusement.// Si nous n'avions pas été hébergés par vous,// nous n'aurions jamais connu // la base de la culture française.// Malgré la brièveté de notre séjour,// nous nous sentons très proches des Français // et emportons avec nous // d'excellents souvenirs d'amitié qui ont créé// des liens très forts entre nous.//

ROBERT: Vous voyez, madame,// c'est exactement ce que je ressens.// Je cherchais mes mots // pour vous dire la même chose.//

MME FOURCHET: Nous gardons aussi // un excellent souvenir de ton séjour.// Combien de fromages // as-tu goûtés chez nous?// Tu t'en souviens?//

ROBERT: Exactement soixante-six,// ou un par jour.//

MME FOURCHET: Alors, il faudra que tu reviennes // pour goûter les deux cent soixante-quatorze qui restent!// Et, en échange, tu nous feras goûter // à la cuisine américaine.// En attendant, mettons-nous à table // et profitons de la bonne chère.//

NARRATOR: Marguerite, Henry et Robert se retrouvent en aparté // avant de passer à table.//

HENRY: Ecoutez, chers amis,// portons un toast à nos progrès en français!// Nous avons tenu notre promesse,// nous n'avons jamais parlé anglais ensemble // et notre français est digne de... //

MARGUERITE: ... digne de tous ceux qui le parlent // dans le monde entier.// A votre santé!//

MARGUERITE, HENRY ET ROBERT: A la nôtre!// A notre prochaine visite en France!//

NARRATOR: A la fin de la soirée,// tous se sont embrassés // et on pouvait entendre la salle résonner // de beaucoup de «au revoir» pleins de nostalgie // et de promesses de s'écrire souvent.//

This is the end of the taped activities for the Chapitre facultatif.

CPSIA information can be obtained at www.ICGtesting.com
Printed in the USA
BVOW04s1654090416

443477BV00003B/22/P

9 781584 657422